BIG ENGLISH 4 PLUS

T0351911

Contents

unit 1

Kids in My Class

1 **Read and look. Write the names.**

Julia is serious. She likes reading. She has got blonde hair.

Tony has got short black hair. He's very friendly and funny.

Amelia has got straight hair. She is shy and plays the flute.

José is friendly and clever. He has got brown hair and wears glasses.

1 _____ 2 _____ 3 _____ 4 _____

2 **Look at 1 and write T for true and F for false.**

1 José wears glasses. _____

2 Amelia has got wavy hair. _____

3 Julia has got brown hair. _____

4 Tony is friendly. _____

5 Amelia is shy. _____

6 Tony is serious. _____

7 José has got black hair. _____

8 Julia likes reading. _____

3 **Listen and write.**

Who's That Girl?

It's the first day of school.
We're back in our classes.
Everybody looks different
And I've got new **¹**_____!

Who's that girl
Standing over there?
She's taller **²**_____ me.
She's got **³**_____ dark hair.

In my class are the same friends I know.
But we all change. We all grow. (x2)

It's the first day of school
And I'm back in my chair.
Everybody looks different.
Now I've got **⁴**_____ hair.

Who's that girl?
Oh, wait, that's Marie!
Last time I saw her,
She was **⁵**_____ than me!

Chorus

4 **Write sentences about two classmates.**

Classmate 1: _____

_____

_____

Classmate 2: _____

_____

_____

5 **Read. Then circle Amanda or Christina.**

She's Just Like You!

There's a new girl in Christina's class at school. Her name is Amanda. She's got curly hair like Christina. But Christina's hair is shorter and curlier than Amanda's. Christina is taller than Amanda. They're both nice and they're both clever but Amanda is shy. Christina definitely isn't. Christina and Amanda are different in some ways but they've got a lot in common.

1 **Amanda / Christina** is a new student.

2 **Amanda / Christina** has got curlier hair.

3 **Amanda / Christina** has got longer hair.

4 **Amanda / Christina** is taller.

5 **Amanda / Christina** is shy.

6 **Think about a classmate. Answer the questions.**

1 What's his/her name? _____

2 What colour is his/her hair? _____

3 Is he/she tall or short? _____

4 Is his/her hair long or short? _____

THINK BIG **Think about a person in your family. Write about how you are the same and how you are different.** _____

_____

_____

7 **Listen and stick.**

Donna

Maddie

Joseph

Henry

Sandra

8 **Complete the sentences.**

1 Maddie is _____ Henry. (tall)

2 Valerie's legs are _____ my legs. (long)

3 My mum's hair is _____ my hair. (wavy)

4 My school is _____ my brother's. (big)

5 This book is _____ that one. (small)

6 Jon's eyes are _____ his dad's eyes. (light)

9 **Look at 8 and complete new sentences.**

1 Henry is _____ Maddie.

2 My legs are _____ Valerie's.

3 My hair is _____ my mum's.

4 My brother's school is _____ my school.

5 That book is _____ this one.

6 His dad's eyes are _____ Jon's.

Language in Action

10 **Read and match.**

1 Bob's friends are older than **our friends**.   mine

2 Our backpacks are heavier than **their backpacks**.   yours

3 Your father is taller than **my father**.   hers

4 José's hair is straighter than **his sister's hair**.   his

5 My eyes are darker than **your eyes**.   ours

6 Kim's backpack is brighter than **her dad's**.   theirs

11 **Complete the sentences.**

1 Juan's hair is short. **Kate's hair** is long.

   Juan's hair is _____ hers.

2 Your class has got 12 students. It's small. **Their class** has got 15 students.

   Your class is _____.

3 His cousin is four feet tall. **My cousin** is only three feet tall.

   His cousin is _____.

4 **Our car** is big but your car is very big. Your car is

   _____.

5 **Your hair** is black. His hair is brown. His hair is

   _____.

6 **His book** is light. Her book is heavier. Her book is

   _____.

7 **Their toys** are good. My toys are very good. My toys are

   _____.

8 His singing is bad. **Her singing** is good. His singing is

   _____.

12 **Complete the sentences.**

> chance   common   fraternal   identical   triplets

1 A mother gave birth to Maria and Martin together. They don't look alike. They are _____ twins.

2 A mother gave birth to Tina, Gina and Nina together. They are _____ .

3 A mother gave birth to Bob and Rob together. They look the same. They are _____ twins.

4 Fraternal twins are more _____ than identical twins.

5 The _____ of having triplets is 1 in every 625 births.

13 **Listen, read and circle. Which animal can have the most babies at one time?**

1   Some scientists say the chance of having **¹fraternal / identical** quadruplets is only 1 in 13 million. Not if you're a nine-banded armadillo! These armadillo mums give birth to up to 56 pups in their lifetime. And every time they give birth, they have FOUR identical babies at a time. That means that an average armadillo has a record-breaking fourteen sets of **²triplets / quadruplets**. That's impossible for humans and very **³rare / common** in the animal kingdom.

nine-banded armadillo

2   **⁴Multiple / Single** births are very common in the animal kingdom. Often, this is because not all the babies survive. Cats usually give birth to 3–5 kittens and some dogs have 5–10 puppies. These little brothers and sisters look alike, just like brothers and sisters in human multiple births, but they're very rarely identical.

3   Other animals rarely or never have multiple births. Usually, **⁵smaller / bigger** animals have more babies and larger animals have fewer. Elephants have only one baby at a time. Whales almost always have only one baby at a time. These animals have a very different relationship with their offspring.

4   However, pigs are different. They're larger than other farm animals but they have lots of babies. Sometimes they have 20 piglets at a time!

14 **Look at 13 and choose the correct answers.**

1 Nine-banded armadillos always have...

    a identical quadruplets.   **b** fraternal quadruplets.

2 How many times does a nine-banded armadillo give birth in its lifetime?

    a 14   **b** 56

3 Which animal never has triplets?

    a an elephant   **b** a cat

4 Which animals usually have more babies?

    a small animals   **b** big animals

5 Which animal almost always has only one baby at a time?

    a a dog   **b** a whale

6 Pigs are unusual because...

    a they don't have multiple births.   **b** they have many babies at once.

15 **Read and write.**

| alike | birth | fingerprints | rare | relationship | survive |

1 You and your brother don't look _____. He's much darker than you.

2 Red hair is very _____ now – not many people have got it.

3 Identical twins aren't completely identical. They've got different _____.

4 Pigs sometimes give _____ to 20 piglets.

5 Small animals have multiple births because they want some of them to _____.

6 The _____ between twins begins before they're born.

THNK BIG **Number in order from 1 (most common) to 5 (least common).**

triplets ☐   identical twins ☐   quadruplets ☐

one baby ☐   fraternal twins ☐

16 **Read and choose the correct answers.**

1 Multiple births are _____ in humans than in animals.

   a more rare than   **b** rarer

2 Is a big lunch _____ a big dinner?

   a healthier than   **b** more healthy

3 Whales _____ than cats and dogs.

   a more are ancient   **b** are more ancient

4 Brown bread is _____ white bread.

   a good for you than   **b** better for you than

5 Car journeys are _____ motorbike journeys.

   a comfortable than   **b** more comfortable than

6 My relationship with my sister _____ with my brother!

   a is worse than   **b** is bad

17 **Look, choose and write.**

The Beach Majestic	
Comfort ★★★★★	Friendly service ★★★★
Food ★★★	Beach safety for children ★★★★
Size of rooms ★★	Cost ★★★★★
Activities ★	

The Beach Comber	
Comfort ★★★	Friendly service ★
Food ★★★★	Beach safety for children –
Size of rooms ★★★★	Cost ★★★
Activities ★★★	

1 The Beach Majestic is _____ the Beach Comber. (comfortable)

2 The food at the Beach Comber is _____ at the Beach Majestic. (good)

3 The rooms at the Beach Comber are _____ at the Beach Majestic. (big)

4 The activities at the Beach Comber are _____ at the Beach Majestic. (interesting)

5 The people at the Beach Majestic are _____ at the Beach Comber. (friendly)

6 The beach at the Beach Comber is _____ at the Beach Majestic. (dangerous)

7 The Beach Majestic is _____ the Beach Comber. (expensive)

Grammar

18 Look at 17. Write five sentences about the hotels. Use the words from the box.

> bad   boring   cheap   safe   uncomfortable

1 _____

2 _____

3 _____

4 _____

5 _____

19 Complete the sentences. Use **more ... than**.

> beautiful   common   expensive   popular   unusual

1 Twins are _____ triplets.

2 Identical triplets are _____ identical twins.

3 The name Kate is _____ the name Astrid now.

4 Ferraris are _____ Volkswagens. They cost a lot.

5 Curly hair looks _____ straight hair. She looks amazing!

20 Use the correct form of the words to make sentences. Make sure the facts are correct.

1 mosquitoes/dangerous/snakes

_____

2 planes/safe/cars

_____

3 orange juice/bad for your teeth/sweets

_____

4 The Harry Potter films/scary/the Madagascar films

_____

5 trainers/comfortable/boots

_____

21 **Read and choose the correct answers.**

1 Hair under your mouth and on your chin is called a

   a beard.   **b** moustache.   **c** hairstyle.

2 The hair between your nose and your mouth is called a

   a hairstyle.   **b** beard.   **c** moustache.

3 The way you cut your hair is called a

   a beard.   **b** hairstyle.   **c** moustache.

22 **Match to make true facts.**

1 The ancient Greeks thought men with beards

2 Prehistoric men didn't shave

3 Beards aren't very popular

4 All Alexander the Great's men

5 In Europe, beards

a in Asia and South America.

b are quite fashionable at the moment.

c because beards looked scarier.

d looked cleverer.

e shaved their beards.

23 **Listen, read and write.**

| beards | categories | competition | fashion | Germany | Moustache |

Some people don't follow ¹_____. There was a group of men like this in ²_____. They didn't want to shave off their beards. Instead, they wanted to grow stranger or more unusual ³_____ than anybody else. They also wanted to compare their special beards and moustaches with other men. They started a ⁴_____ in the 1990s. At first, it was only for German men. But soon, men from other countries, like the United States, Norway and Switzerland, also started competing. It became the World Beard and ⁵_____ Championship. Now, there is a championship every two years. Today, the competition has got sixteen different ⁶_____.

24 **Look at 23. Circle T for true and F for false.**

1 The competition started in the United States.   T   F

2 In the competition, men compare beards and moustaches.   T   F

3 Men from Norway and Switzerland compete in the championship.   T   F

4 The championship is every two years.   T   F

5 There are eight different categories.   T   F

6 The men in the competition are very fashionable.   T   F

25 **Read and match.**

1 This man's beard looks like a star. He's competing in the Freestyle Beard category.

a

2 This man has got a long English Moustache. It's white and goes out at the sides.

b

3 This man is competing in the Verdi category. He's got a white beard and a curly moustache.

c

4 Look at this man's moustache! It's long and curls up. He looks like the famous painter, Salvador Dalí.

d

 THINK BIG

Choose a new category for the World Beard and Moustache Championship. Describe it.

Category: _____

Description: _____

26 **Read and number the parts of the paragraph.**

My Best Friend ← ——————————————— 1

My best friend's name is James. ← ——————————— 2

He's shorter than me and his hair is darker than mine. James is shy and he is ← — 3
funny, too. We like playing football at the weekend.

I'm happy to have a friend like James. ← ——————————— 4

a detail sentences ☐   **b** final sentence ☐

c title ☐   **d** topic sentence ☐

27 **Read the paragraph. Circle the detail sentences. Copy the topic and final sentences.**

Mr Smith is my favourite teacher. He's the music teacher at my school. He can sing! He also plays the piano and the guitar. He's also very clever and he is funny, too. I'm happy to have a teacher like Mr Smith.

Topic sentence: _____

_____

Final sentence: _____

_____

28 **Look at 27. Write about a favourite teacher.**

Topic sentence: _____

Detail 1: _____

Detail 2: _____

Detail 3: _____

Final sentence: _____

29 **Read and circle ear and air.**

> year   fair   skirt
>
> curly   pair   hear
>
> chair   taller
>
> hair   fear   more

30 **Underline the words with ear and air. Then read aloud.**

1 She's got small ears and curly fair hair.

2 I hear a pair of twins near the stairs.

31 **Connect the letters. Then write.**

1 y   air   **a** _ _ _ _ _

2 ch   ear   **b** _ _ _ _

32 **Listen and write.**

A boy with big ¹ _____

And ² _____ hair,

Hears the twins on the

³ _____.

A boy with big ears and fair

⁴ _____,

⁵ _____ the twins sit on

Their chairs.

33 **Read and match.**

1 Twins are the

2 Identical twins look

3 Triplets are more

4 Quadruplets are

a very rare.

b common than quadruplets.

c most common.

d the same.

34 **Look and complete the sentences.**

glasses   serious
shorter   straight
taller   wavy

1 Mum's hair is _____.

2 Dad's hair is _____.

3 Mia is _____ than Tim.

4 Tim is _____ than Mia.

5 Grandma wears _____.

6 Mia likes to read. She is _____.

35 **Rewrite the sentences.**

My hair is longer than yours.

His hair is shorter than mine.

1 My hair is longer than yours.
Your hair is shorter
_____.

2 Your brother is taller than mine.
My brother is shorter
_____.

3 His hair is curlier than hers.
Her hair is straighter
_____.

4 Her legs are shorter than his.
His legs are longer
_____.

5 Our car is cheaper than theirs.
Their car is more expensive
_____.

6 Their house is smaller than ours.
Our house is bigger
_____.

unit 2 Our Schedule

1 **Look and write.**

> eat   go (x3)   have   visit

1 _____

2 _____

3 _____

4 _____

5 _____

6 _____

2 **Read and write the verbs.**

1 How often do you _____ to the dentist? I go twice a year.

2 I love going to restaurants so I _____ out once a month.

3 When we _____ on holiday, we love eating out.

4 My grandparents now live in Spain so we only _____ them in the summer and winter holidays.

5 Weddings are great fun but I don't _____ to them very often.

6 At my cousin's wedding I'm playing the guitar. I have to _____ lots of guitar lessons before the day!

3 Listen and circle.

Things We Do!

There are lots and lots of things
That I do every day,
Like go to school, **have / watch** a film,
Stay up late and play!

But there are lots of other things
I don't want to do so much,
Like **go / see** to the dentist, **make / do** the dishes,
Make / Do my bed and such.

How often do you do these things?
Every day? Once a week? Once a year?

I **take in / take out** the rubbish
On Tuesdays before school.
And I feed our funny cat
But I don't mind – she's cool.

Chorus

4 What about you? Complete the chart.

once a day	I _____
twice a day	I _____
every night	I _____
every summer	I _____

5 **Read. Then circle.**

A Lot of Weddings!

Christina and Amanda are talking about their plans for the weekend. Amanda is going to her grandma's house. She visits her grandma every week. Christina is going to her cousin's wedding. She goes to weddings three times a year. Christina doesn't like weddings because she has to wear a dress.

1 Amanda is going to her **cousin's / grandma's** house.

2 Amanda sees her grandma once a **week / month**.

3 Christina is going to her **brother's / cousin's** wedding.

4 Christina goes to three weddings a **year / week**.

6 **Now answer the questions about you.**

1 How often do you visit your grandma? _____

2 How often do you go to weddings? _____

3 What are you doing this weekend? _____

THINK BIG **Think and write in order.**

every day every Friday once a year
three times a month twice a day

not very often ➤ _____ ➤ _____ ➤ _____ ➤ _____ ➤ very often

_____ _____ _____ _____

_____ _____ _____ _____

7 **Listen and stick. Number in order.**

a

b

c

d

8 **Circle the correct words.**

1 **What / Where** are they doing after school?

2 **What / Where** is she doing tomorrow?

3 **What / Where** are they going now?

4 **What / Where** is he doing after school?

5 **What / Where** are you doing on Saturday evening?

6 **What / Where** are we going on holiday?

9 **Look at the questions in 8. Match. Then write the answers. Use the words from the box.**

eat out   go (x4)   visit

a ☐ They _____ on holiday.

b ☐ He _____ his cousins.

c ☐ She _____ to her uncle's wedding.

d ☐ We _____ to China.

e ☐ They _____ to the dentist.

f ☐ I _____ with my parents.

Language in Action

10 Look at Laura's schedule. Answer the questions.

This is my schedule.

| every day | once a week |
| twice a day | twice a week |

	Sun	Mon	Tue	Wed	Thu	Fri	Sat
play outside	✓	✓	✓	✓	✓	✓	✓
brush teeth	✓✓	✓✓	✓✓	✓✓	✓✓	✓✓	✓✓
take out the rubbish					✓		
have piano lessons		✓		✓			

1 How often does Laura play outside? _____

2 How often does Laura brush her teeth? _____

3 How often does Laura take out the rubbish? _____

4 How often does Laura have piano lessons? _____

11 Read and match. Then complete.

1 What are you doing this weekend?

a About _____ a week.

2 How often do you eat pizza?

b They're _____ to the zoo.

3 Where are they going this afternoon?

c I'm going _____ visit my friend.

12 **Read and match.**

1 Lucy's got lots of friends.

2 Paul's good-looking.

3 This song goes with an advert.

4 This is something I buy.

5 These are big posters by the side of the road.

6 This makes you want to buy something.

a It's a product.

b It's a jingle.

c He's attractive.

d They're billboards.

e An advertisement.

f She's popular.

 13 31 **Listen, read and circle. What do children love?**

Advertising

Buy it now! Only €2.99

Washes whiter and faster

Adele's favourite cereal

For a healthy and happy life

When big companies are going to make an advert, they use four things to make us buy.

1 For cereals and children's food, they create a cartoon ¹**character** / **person**. Children love them. When children see them, they want to buy!

2 For important products like trainers, coffee and perfume, they choose ²**famous** / **well-known** actors or sports people. We like to buy the things that these people use.

3 Companies use other ³**tools** / **tunes** for selling, too. Things we can read or hear. For example, they use ⁴**slogans** / **advertisements**. They're catchy phrases we can't forget when we think about a product.

4 Companies also use clever images with ⁵**bright** / **attractive** colours and interesting photos. Exciting billboards help sell products because they catch our ⁶**eye** / **nose** and make us think about the product.

 14 **Look at 13. Read and write.**

| buy | cereal | forget | images |

1 Cartoons help sell _____ to children.

2 We like to _____ the products sports people use.

3 When a slogan is good, we can't _____ the words.

4 Clever _____ on billboards help sell products.

15 **Look at the advert. Read and circle T for true and F for false.**

1 This advert uses a cartoon character to sell the product.   **T**   **F**

2 It uses a jingle to help you remember the product.   **T**   **F**

3 It tells you it will make you popular.   **T**   **F**

16 **Complete the sentences. Use the words from the box.**

> catch   company   slogan   tune

1 I like that _____. I can't stop singing it!

2 Your dress is amazing. It's going to _____ everyone's eye!

3 My dad works for a big drinks _____ in New York.

4 The _____ for their drinks is 'The taste you have in mind'. That's very clever.

Would you buy 123 juice? Why/Why not? Use some of the words from the box.

> attractive   bright   famous   jingle   name   popular   product

I would/wouldn't buy 123 juice because _____

_____.

17 **Complete the sentences. Use the words from the box.**

Are   going   is   isn't   not   to

1 It's _____ to be cold later. Take a jumper with you.

2 Francesca _____ going to wear a dress because she hasn't got one.

3 We're going _____ travel to the island by boat.

4 _____ you going to visit Disneyworld in Orlando?

5 I'm _____ going to watch TV this evening. I've got too much homework!

6 Zoe _____ going to study Chemistry in Edinburgh next year.

18 **Complete the email. Use going to. Who's going to get married?**

From: siennac@imac.com

To: jbruno@doodle.co.us

Subject: Martha's wedding

Hi Jessie,

How are you?

I ¹_____ (not be) at Anita's house on

Thursday. I ²_____ (help) Mum

and Dad. My sister Martha is getting married this weekend and they

³_____ (have) the wedding party in

our garden. We ⁴_____ (put) a big

tent in the garden for all the people. Mum and my aunties

⁵_____ (make) all the food. Dad says it

⁶_____ (not rain) but you never know!

⁷_____ (you/come) to the wedding? It

⁸_____ (be) brilliant.

Hope you can come.

Love,

Sienna

19 **Read and write about the concert. Use going to.**

> **Plans for concert – Saturday 25th July**
> 1 play music – Gail, Tom, Sam
> 2 take photos for posters – ~~Harry~~ Craig and Dan
> 3 make the advertising posters - Fran
> 4 put up the posters around the town – ~~Gaby and Marie~~ Rob
> 5 get the garden ready – Gaby and Harry
> 6 Tickets €1

1 _____

2 _____

3 _____

4 _____

5 _____

6 _____

20 **Write the questions.**

1 What/do/on Saturday?

_____

2 Where/go/on Sunday?

_____

3 What time/go to bed/on Friday night?

_____

4 Who/see/at the weekend?

_____

5 the weather/be good/this week?

_____

6 Where/go/for your holidays/next summer?

_____

21 **Read and match.**

1 What's the capital of Japan?

2 Where's Libya?

3 What's a good job for book lovers?

4 Where can you usually see cows?

5 What kind of doors do you find in Japan?

6 Where can you cool off in a hot country?

a Sliding ones.

b On a farm.

c In the shower.

d In Africa.

e A librarian.

f It's Tokyo.

 34 **22** **Listen and read. Then listen again and match.**

a three times a day

c twice a day

e never

b every day

d every morning

f every week

 http://www.unusualhabits.com

What unusual habits have you got?

 ABC_girl Listen to this! I always put the books on my shelf in alphabetical order and I HAVE to check them ¹_____.

 birdsong I live in Libya, Africa. It's REALLY hot all year. So I have a shower ² _____ because it makes me feel clean and cool!

 racerXYZ I've got a weird habit. I ³ _____ touch doorknobs. I really like sliding doors because they haven't got doorknobs. It's lucky that I live in Tokyo, Japan.

 snowflake My habits aren't that strange, apart from one. I always drink COLD milk. I drink it ⁴ _____, ALWAYS with ice. I love our milk in Hertfordshire, England. It's delicious.

 hatman22 I wear a hat ⁵ _____ to school. I even wear it in bed AND in the shower! It's cold here – in Rio Grande, Argentina.

 tbear02 Guess how many toy animals I've got on my bed? Fifty. They're all different shapes and sizes. I always put them in exactly the same place ⁶ _____ after I make my bed. But I'm not crazy.

23 **Look at 22. Read and choose the correct answers.**

1 ABC_girl puts her books...

    a under her bed.   **b** in a library.   **c** in a special order.

2 birdsong has showers because...

    a he feels clean.   **b** it's fun.   **c** he's too hot.

3 Where is racerXYZ from?

    a Scotland   **b** Japan   **c** England

4 What does snowflake drink every day?

    a cola   **b** milk   **c** water

5 What's the weather like in Rio Grande?

    a It's warm.   **b** It's cool.   **c** It's cold.

6 What does hatman22 wear in bed and in the shower?

    a hat   **b** coat   **c** gloves

7 tbear02's toys are always...

    a the same size   **b** near her bed   **c** in the same place

8 Who thinks he/she isn't crazy?

    a hatman22   **b** ABC_girl   **c** tbear02

24 **Circle the odd one out.**

1 bookshelf   habit   doorknob   bed

2 strange   cool   unusual   weird

3 make the bed   touch the knob   tidy my room   put the books in order

25 **Match the descriptions to the word groups in 24.**

a doing housework   ☐

b words with the same meaning   ☐

c furniture and things in a house   ☐

THINK BIG

What do you do every day, week or month that's strange or unusual and why?

Every day/week/month, I _____

because _____ .

26 **Read and circle the sequence words.**

> **My Day at School**
> First, we've got a Maths lesson. Next, we've got a spelling test. Then we have lunch. After that, we've got an English lesson. Finally, we've got a P.E. lesson.

27 **Read the paragraph. Look at 26. Write the sequence words.**

I am busy after school. ¹_____,
I have a snack. ²_____, I walk my
dog. ³_____ I play outside.
⁴_____, I eat dinner.
⁵_____, I do the dishes with my
brother and dad.

28 **What do you do after school? Add two more activities. Then number the six activities in order. Write a paragraph.**

☐ do homework   ☐ have a snack   ☐ _____

☐ eat dinner   ☐ play games   ☐ _____

_____

_____

_____

_____

_____

_____

29 **Read and circle ir and ur.**

bird   shirt   fur
dear   stairs   curl
ear   hurt   skirt
girl   surf

30 **Underline the words with ir and ur. Then read aloud.**

1 The girl is wearing a short skirt and a long T-shirt.

2 Pandas have got black and white fur.

31 **Connect the letters. Then write.**

1	s	urn	**a** _ _ _ _
2	t	urf	**b** _ _ _ _
3	b	urt	**c** _ _ _ _
4	h	ird	**d** _ _ _ _

32 **Listen and write.**

39

Two ¹_____ with red
²_____,
Two cats with black ³_____,
Two boys with white ⁴_____,
Are watching ⁵_____!

33 **Complete the dialogue.**

Ana: Hey, José! ¹_____ are you doing after school?

José: I'm really busy. ²_____, I'm visiting my grandmother.

Ana: Then what are you going ³_____?

José: Then I'm meeting my mum.

Ana: ⁴_____ are you going?

José: We're ⁵_____ to the dentist.

Ana: Oh, no.

José: That's okay. ⁶_____, we ⁷_____ going to the cinema!

34 **Write the questions using How often. Then answer using the words from the box.**

| do the dishes/twice a week | go on holiday/twice a year |
| play outside/every day | watch a DVD/once a week |

1

_____?

He _____.

2

_____?

_____

3

_____?

_____

4

_____?

_____

Food Around the World

 unit 3

1 **Match. Write the letter.**

1 _____ porridge	**a**	**b**	**2** _____ steamed buns
3 _____ paella	**c**	**d**	**4** _____ watermelon
5 _____ toasted cheese sandwich	**e**	**f**	**6** _____ cereal with milk
7 _____ lamb meatballs	**g**	**h**	**8** _____ noodle soup

 2 **What food do you like?**

Breakfast: _____

Lunch: _____

Dinner: _____

3 **Listen and number in order. Which food is in the song? Tick (✓) or cross (✗).**

Would You Like Some?

"Come on, Sam. Just one little bite!"
"Oh, really, Dad. Oh, all right!
Mmm. Hey, you're right. It's great!
Please put some more on my plate!"

Come on, Sam, please have a little taste!
Come on, Sam, don't make a funny face!

"Would you like some chicken curry?"
"No thanks, Dad. I'm in a hurry!"
Sam says, "No, Dad, not right now
But thanks so much – thanks, anyhow."

"How about a sweet steamed bun?
It's really yummy. Come on, try one!"
Sam says, "No, Dad, not right now
But thanks so much – thanks, anyhow."

Chorus

"Would you like some noodle soup?
Tonight it tastes really nice!"
Sam says, "No, Dad, not right now
But thanks so much – thanks, anyhow."

4 **Correct the strange food and write.**

1 steamed watermelon   _____

2 porridge curry   _____

3 toasted yoghurt sandwich   _____

4 apple soup   _____

5 cereal with lemonade   _____

5 **Read. Then write T for true and F for false.**

Homemade Lemonade

Sam makes some cake and lemonade. He asks Christina to try them. Christina tries some cake but she doesn't like it. Then she tries the lemonade but it's horrible. It's too sour! Christina asks Sam what he put in the lemonade. He put in lemons, water and ice but he forgot the sugar!

1 Christina likes Sam's cake.   _____

2 Christina thinks the lemonade tastes good.   _____

3 The lemonade is sweet.   _____

4 Sam put lemons in his lemonade.   _____

5 Sam forgot to put sugar in his lemonade.   _____

6 **Write about you. Answer Yes, I would or No, I wouldn't.**

1 Would you like to drink some lemon juice?   _____

2 Would you like to eat some chocolate cake?   _____

3 Would you like to drink some lemonade?   _____

THINK BIG **What happens next in the story? Write.**

_____

_____

7 **Listen and stick. Do they like the food? Tick (✓) or cross (✗).**

1  ☐   **2** ☐   **3** ☐    **4** ☐

8 **Look and complete the questions and answers. Use would like.**

Linda

Drinks
lemonade ☐
apple juice ☐
milk ✓

Lunch
lamb meatballs ☐
noodle soup ✓
steamed buns ☐

Paul

Drinks
lemonade ✓
apple juice ☐
milk ☐

Lunch
lamb meatballs ✓
noodle soup ☐
steamed buns ✓

Maria

Drinks
lemonade ☐
apple juice ✓
milk ☐

Lunch
lamb meatballs ☐
noodle soup ☐
steamed buns ☐

1 What _____ Linda _____?

_____

2 What _____ Paul _____?

_____

3 What _____ Maria _____?

_____

Language in Action

9 **Look at the pictures. Complete the sentences.**

1

A: _____ she _____ to have some pasta?

B: _____, she _____.

2

A: _____ he _____ to eat some porridge?

B: _____, he _____.

3

A: _____ they _____ to drink watermelon milkshakes?

B: _____, they _____.

4

A: _____ they _____ to try some curry?

B: _____, they _____.

10 **Complete for you.**

1 _____ you _____ to try _____?
Yes, I _____.

2 _____ you _____ to try _____?
No, I _____.

3 _____ your friend _____ to try _____?
Yes, he/she _____. No, he/she _____.

11 **Circle the correct words.**

1 For **a balanced** / **an unhealthy** diet, eat food from each of the five food groups every day.

2 The five food groups are: fruit, vegetables, dairy, protein and **chicken** / **grains**.

3 Eat more **vegetables** / **dairy** than protein.

4 Don't eat food that is too **tasty** / **salty**.

5 Don't have too many **sugary** / **watery** drinks.

6 **Wholemeal** / **Diet** bread is healthier than white bread.

12 **Listen, read and complete. Which food can be both low- and full-fat?**

| balance | bigger | five | grains | guide | smaller | sugar |

1   We need to eat a balanced diet. That means we should eat foods from each of the ¹_____ food groups every day. The main food groups are grains, vegetables, fruit, protein and dairy.

2   Look at the 'My Plate' picture. This shows the amount of each food group we should eat. It's very important to get the right ²_____.

3   The vegetables section is ³_____ than all the others, so we should eat more of them than any other food. The ⁴_____ section is also very important. We need to eat a little more of them than protein. Fruit is also important but it's got lots of ⁵_____, so we can't eat too much of it. And dairy foods aren't always low-fat. A lot of dairy foods can actually make us fat. That's why the dairy section is ⁶_____ than all the others.

4   Would you like to be healthier? Then remember to always use 'My Plate' as a ⁷_____ at mealtimes.

My Plate
Fruit Grains Dairy
Vegetables Protein

13 **Look at 12. Circle T for true and F for false.**

1 We don't need to eat all five food groups every day.   T   F

2 Put mostly protein on your plate.   T   F

3 It's bad to eat too much fruit.   T   F

4 Fruit isn't sugary but it's fatty.   T   F

5 It's better to eat low-fat dairy foods.   T   F

6 'My Plate' is a very useful guide.   T   F

14 **Match the words and definitions.**

1 This is the word we use for all the foods we choose to eat.

2 We describe crisps and chips with this word.

3 We describe sweets, cakes and cola with this word.

4 Chicken and fish are healthy sources of this.

5 Cheese contains a lot of this.

a fat

b protein

c salty

d diet

e sugary

15 **Write the food on the plate.**

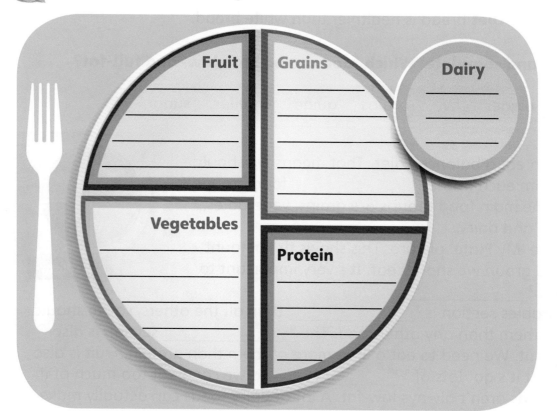

| bananas |
| beans |
| bread |
| carrots |
| cereal |
| cheese |
| chicken |
| fish |
| mangoes |
| milk |
| oranges |
| pasta |
| peppers |
| potatoes |
| rice |
| yoghurt |

THINK BIG

Who has the most balanced diet? Read and complete.

John has cereal with milk, a mango, a chicken sandwich, a salad and a yoghurt.

Jenny has a cheese and pepperoni pizza, a yoghurt, a glass of milk and some crisps.

¹_____ has a balanced diet. ²_____ doesn't have a balanced diet. He/She eats too much ³_____ and ⁴_____ and not enough ⁵_____, ⁶_____ or ⁷_____.

16 **Put the words in order.**

1 dinner | we | shall | now? | have

_____

2 can | go | I | to | party? | Kim's

_____

3 café. | go | that | let's | to

_____

4 Martin | visit | can | tonight? | us

_____

5 people? | shall | invite | I | a lot of

_____

6 for Francis? | buying | how about | chocolates | some

_____

17 **Match 1–6 in 16 to the answers a–f.**

a No. He doesn't eat sweets.

b Yes. But he can only stay until nine o' clock.

c I don't think that's a good idea. The house is very small.

d Yes, let's. It looks nice.

e No, sorry, you can't. We're visiting Grandma on that day.

f That's a good idea. I'm very hungry.

18 **Write How about, Shall or Let's.**

1 _____ try some typical Spanish food.

2 _____ I make you a nice hot drink?

3 _____ turn on the TV.

4 _____ making some pasta for dinner?

5 _____ we eat out at a restaurant tonight?

6 _____ some chocolate ice cream for dessert?

7 _____ I put an apple in your lunch box?

8 _____ using 'My Plate' as your guide?

Grammar

19 **Read and choose the correct answers.**

Tamsin: It's Harry's birthday on Saturday.

Kim: Oh yes, I forgot! ¹_____ we surprise him with a party?

Tamsin: Oh no, he wouldn't like that but ²_____ making him a cake?

Kim: That's a good idea. ³_____ help you make it?

Tamsin: Yes, that would be great. ⁴_____ make it at my house or your house?

Kim: Oh, I'm not sure. ⁵_____ ask my mum. Mum! ⁶_____ Tamsin and I make a cake for Harry today?

Mum: Yes, of course ⁷_____. I've got some great recipes for vegetable cakes with carrots and peppers.

Kim: That's really kind, Mum. But ⁸_____ just make a simple chocolate cake, please?

Mum: Oh yes, sorry!

1	**a** Let's	**b** Shall	**c** Can I
2	**a** how about	**b** let's	**c** can we
3	**a** Can he	**b** Shall I	**c** Let's
4	**a** Shall we	**b** Let's	**c** How about
5	**a** How about	**b** Can	**c** Let's
6	**a** Shall	**b** Can	**c** Let's
7	**a** can	**b** you shall	**c** you can
8	**a** can we	**b** how about	**c** let

20 **Complete the sentences.**

> lunch box   main meal   Organic food   school canteen

1 In the UK, pupils don't eat in their classrooms – they eat in the
_____.

2 In some countries, lunch is the _____ of the day.

3 _____ grows naturally – without chemicals.

4 Some Japanese children bring their food to school in a
_____.

21 **Read and circle. Which is bigger in Brazil: lunch or dinner?**

1   In Brazil, our school lunches are ¹ **small** / **big** and healthy. For most people in Brazil, lunch is bigger than breakfast or dinner. It's the main ² **meal** / **dinner** of the day. That's why it's important to have a good meal at school!

2   We usually eat in the ³ **classroom** / **school canteen**. It's a ⁴ **hot** / **cold** meal, with either meat or fish. We also eat ⁵ **yoghurt** / **fruit** and vegetables and usually some bread. However, the main part of the meal is almost always ⁶ **pasta** / **rice** and beans.

3   The food we have at lunchtime comes from farms near our school. I don't know if the food is organic but it's fresh and our meals are balanced.

22 **Look at 21. Write yes or no.**

1 Lunch in Brazil is a healthy and balanced meal.   _____

2 They eat beans and rice every day.   _____

3 Food is always organic.   _____

4 The food for lunch comes from far away.   _____

5 They eat meat or fish for lunch.   _____

THINK BIG

Which meal should be bigger: breakfast, lunch or dinner?
Put them in order, starting with the smallest. Why?

1 _____   2 _____   3 _____

_____

_____

23 **Read about school lunches on pages 46 and 47 of your Pupil's Book. Then write about *your* school lunches. What's the same/different?**

What do they eat for lunch in England?

Japan	_____ (my country)	Same or Different?
Children take turns serving.		
Children eat lunch in their classroom.		
England		
Most children bring sandwiches from home.		
Dinner is the main meal of the day.		
Zambia		
People often eat the same thing for lunch and dinner.		
People eat some food with their hands.		
Italy		
Food is often organic.		
Children eat meat for lunch once or twice a week.		

24 **Read and write so or because.**

1 I love eating paella _____ I have it twice a week.

2 I don't like eating chicken curry _____ I don't like spicy food.

25 **Match and circle the conjunctions.**

1 She doesn't like milk   **a** so we eat them every week.

2 It's cold today   **b** because I want to be healthy.

3 I often have a toasted cheese sandwich for breakfast   **c** so I'm having porridge for breakfast.

4 We love eating meatballs   **d** because he's Spanish.

5 Carlos likes paella   **e** so she doesn't drink it.

6 I eat a balanced diet   **f** because I like cheese a lot.

26 **Join the sentences and write. Use so and because.**

1 I'm wearing a coat. It's cold.

_____

2 I don't like fruit. I don't eat watermelon.

_____

3 Sally is happy. She's eating her favourite lunch.

_____

27 **Read and circle le, el, al and il.**

apple   curl   pupil

pencil   medal   sandal

hear   camel   hair

bubble   travel

28 **Underline the words with le, el, al and il. Then read aloud.**

1 There are apples in April.

2 I wear sandals when I travel in summer.

29 **Connect the letters. Then write.**

1	app	el	**a** _ _ _ _ _
2	pup	le	**b** _ _ _ _ _
3	cam	al	**c** _ _ _ _ _
4	med	il	**d** _ _ _ _ _

30 60 **Listen and write.**

Take your ¹_____ .
Draw a ²_____ .
Draw a ³_____ .
Draw some ⁴_____ .

31 **Write questions or answers.**

1 What would she like for breakfast?

_____

2 _____

He'd like a toasted cheese sandwich for lunch.

3 What would they like for dinner?

_____

4 _____

They'd like chicken curry for dinner.

5 What would you like for dinner?

_____

32 **Read and circle.**

Mum: ¹ **Would / Shall** you like to go to an Indian restaurant?

Bobby: No, I ² **can't / wouldn't**.

Mum: ³ **Let's / How about** an Italian restaurant?

Bobby: No, ⁴ **let's / thanks**.

Mum: Well. Where ⁵ **can / would** you like to go?

Bobby: ⁶ **I'd like / Let's go** to a sweet shop!

33 **Read and match.**

1 Eat more grains
2 Don't eat too
3 Have lots of
4 Have a

a balanced diet.
b much salt.
c than protein.
d fruit.

My Robot

1 **Choose and draw one path. Design a robot.**

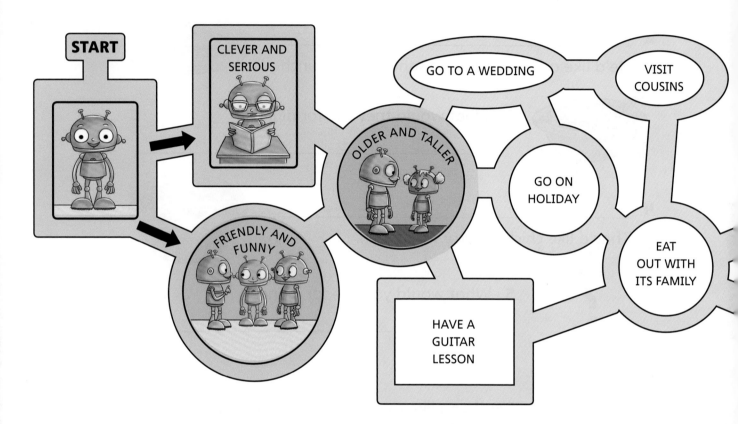

START

CLEVER AND SERIOUS

OLDER AND TALLER

FRIENDLY AND FUNNY

GO TO A WEDDING

VISIT COUSINS

GO ON HOLIDAY

EAT OUT WITH ITS FAMILY

HAVE A GUITAR LESSON

2 **Look at your path in 1. Answer the questions with words from your path.**

What is the robot like? _____

What is it doing today? _____

What would it like to try? _____

3 **Look at your path in 1 and ✓ the word or words.**

My robot likes ☐ spicy ☐ salty ☐ sweet ☐ sour food.

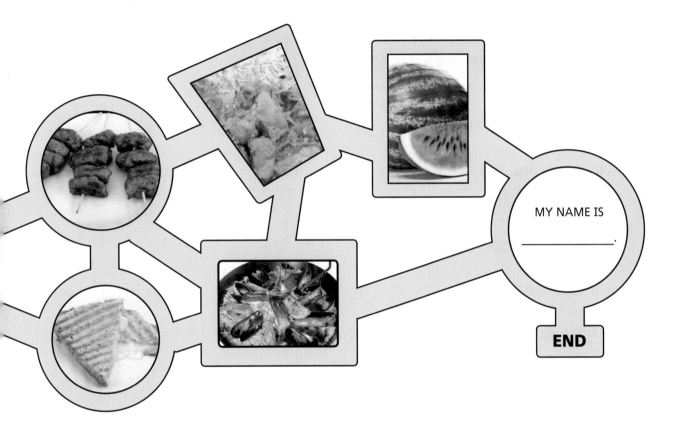

MY NAME IS

_____.

END

4 **Look at the information about your robot. Give it a name. Write a paragraph about it.**

_____

_____

_____

_____

_____

_____

How Do You Feel?

1 **Complete the sentences.**

> allergies   coughing   cut   fever   headache
> sneezing   stomachache   toothache

1 His teeth are sore. He's got a ☐☐☐☐☐Ⓐ☐☐☐ .

2 I've got a cold. I'm ☐☐☐☐☐Ⓞ☐☐ and I feel tired.

3 I've got Ⓞ☐☐☐☐☐☐☐☐☐☐☐ .
I don't want to eat anything.

4 Your dad has got a ☐☐☐☐☐Ⓞ☐☐ . His head is sore.

5 My little sister fell. Now she's got a bad ☐Ⓤ☐ on her leg.

6 Your head feels hot. You must have a ☐☐☐Ⓞ☐ .

7 My mum has got bad ☐Ⓞ☐☐☐☐☐☐☐ . She's
☐☐Ⓞ☐☐☐Ⓞ☐ a lot.

2 **Write the letters from the circles in 1. Use the letters to complete the joke.**

ⓐ ◯ ◯ ◯ ⓤ ◯ ◯ ◯ ◯

Doctor, my son ate my pen! What should I do?

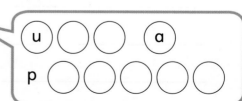

u ◯ ◯ a
p ◯ ◯ ◯ ◯ ◯

3 Listen and write. Use the words from the box.

Stay in Bed and Rest!

You're ¹_____
And you're ²_____.
You need to stay in bed.
I think you've got a fever.
Here, let me feel your head.
You shouldn't go to school today.
You should ³_____ instead.

When you're ill or feeling blue,
Your family takes good care of you.

You've got a ⁴_____
And a ⁵_____.
Here's what I suggest:
You should drink some ⁶_____
And juice.
⁷_____ and rest!
Listen to your dad, now.
Taking care of yourself is best.

Chorus

cold   coughing   fever
sneezing   stay home
Stay in bed   tea

4 Read and choose the correct answers.

When you're ill, here's what I suggest:

1 You shouldn't…

  a stay in bed.   **b** go to school.   **c** stay home.

2 You shouldn't…

  a run around.   **b** rest.   **c** drink water.

3 You shouldn't…

  a go to a doctor.   **b** eat sweets.   **c** take care of yourself.

5 **Read. Then answer the questions.**

You're Hurt!

Sam and Christina are having lunch together. Sam sees something red on Christina's arm. He gets upset because he thinks Christina has got a cut. He tells Christina that she should go to see the nurse and put a plaster on her arm. But Christina tells him that it's not blood on her arm – it's ketchup! She's alright but she needs a napkin.

1 What are Sam and Christina doing? _____

2 Who does Sam think Christina should see? _____

3 What does Sam think Christina should do? _____

6 **Read. Then complete the sentences.**

> nurse   plaster   rest   run

I fell over and cut my knee. Ouch!

You should _____

_____.

_____.

You shouldn't _____.

THINK BIG **Look at 5 again. What happens next in the story? Write.**

_____

_____

71

7 **Listen and stick. Number in order and write.**

a

He should go to the _____.

b

She should go to the _____.

c

She should take some _____.

d

He should eat some soup and
get some _____.

8 **Read and circle.**

1 I **should / shouldn't** eat vegetables.

2 He **should / shouldn't** exercise every day.

3 We **should / shouldn't** stay up late.

4 They **should / shouldn't** eat healthy food.

9 **Read and write should or shouldn't.**

1 **Joe:** I've got a headache.

Doctor: You _____ drink some water.

2 **Dad:** My children have got allergies.

Doctor: They _____ stay inside and take medicine.

3 **Mum:** My son has got a fever.

Doctor: He _____ go to school.

4 **Sonya:** I like watching TV for hours every day.

Doctor: You _____ watch so much TV.

Language in Action

10 **Read and ✓ the correct answers.**

1 I go to bed late and eat lots of crisps. I should take better care of _____.

   a ☐ myself   **b** ☐ yourself   **c** ☐ herself

2 You never eat fruit. You should take better care of _____.

   a ☐ myself   **b** ☐ yourself   **c** ☐ ourselves

3 She does a lot of exercise. She takes good care of _____.

   a ☐ himself   **b** ☐ themselves **c** ☐ herself

4 We eat a healthy breakfast. We take good care of _____.

   a ☐ myself   **b** ☐ ourselves   **c** ☐ themselves

5 They watch TV all the time. They should take better care of _____.

   a ☐ themselves **b** ☐ ourselves   **c** ☐ herself

6 He always washes his hands. He takes good care of _____.

   a ☐ herself   **b** ☐ myself   **c** ☐ himself

11 **Read the problems. Write advice.**

1 I'm coughing and I've got a sore throat.

_____

2 My brother has got a cut on his leg.

_____

3 My friends don't eat vegetables.

_____

4 I've got stomachache.

_____

5 I stay up late every night.

_____

12 **Listen, read and complete. When should we use tissues?**

> clean   dirty water   diseases   enemies
> microscope   protect   spread   toothbrush

1 **About Germs**
We try to stay healthy,
but there are tiny
¹_____ all around us
called germs. They're always there
but we can only see them
with a ²_____.
Unfortunately, they can cause
³_____.

2 **Where Are Germs?**
They're everywhere.
In the air, on old food, in
⁴_____ and on everything
we touch with our hands – the sink,
the bath, our ⁵_____, the
TV remote control and the
computer keyboard.

3 **Kinds of Germs**
There isn't just one kind
of germ, there are at least four.
Each one is a bit different. The
main ones are bacteria, viruses,
fungi and protozoa.

4 **How Do We**
⁶_____ Ourselves?
We can wash our hands
often and keep the house
⁷_____. When we've got
a cold or a cough, we should use
tissues. Also, we should stay at
home, so our germs don't
⁸_____.

13 **Read and answer.**

1 How many kinds of germs are there?   _____

2 Can germs make us ill?   _____

3 Write three ways germs can get into the home.

_____

4 Write three ways we can stay away from germs.

_____

14 **Match. Look at page 64 of the Pupil's Book.**

1 virus

2 bacteria

3 fungi

4 protozoa

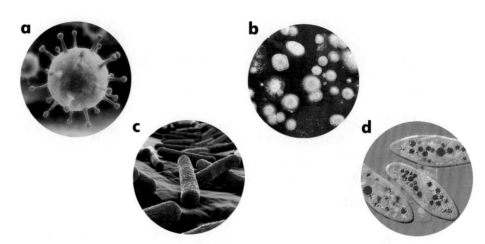

15 **Write germs 1–4 next to the information. Use the text on page 64 of the Pupil's Book.**

1 They grow on old food. _____ _____

2 They live in dirty water. _____

3 It's in the air and gives us coughs and colds. _____

4 The disease malaria comes from this. _____

5 They're sometimes good and help us digest food. _____

6 It can spread quickly through sneezes. _____

THINK BIG

Think and ✓ or ✗. Can you find germs on a...?

library book ☐   computer mouse ☐   toilet ☐   coin ☐

phone ☐   door ☐   toy ☐   water fountain ☐

Which do you think has the most germs? Why?

_____

_____

16 **Read and write questions and short answers with should and shouldn't.**

A

Mum didn't put the meat in the fridge. It was out of the fridge all night!

1 eat/they/the meat?

_____

No, they _____.

2 throw/they/the meat in the bin?

_____

Yes, they _____.

B

Dad has got a really bad cold. But he's got an important meeting at work.

3 go/he/to work?

_____

_____

4 stay/he/at home today?

_____

_____

C

Amalia and Denise found a handbag in the street. They are deciding what to do.

5 keep/we/the handbag?

_____

_____

6 take/we/it to the police?

_____

_____

D

Marlena has got an important exam tomorrow.

7 revise/she/all night?

_____

_____

8 go/she/to bed without revising?

_____

_____

17 **Look at 16 and match A–D to four of the suggestions below. Write sentences with could.**

- give the meat to the cat
- use the computer to take part in the meeting
- eat the meat tonight
- look for a phone number in the handbag
- get up early and revise
- give the handbag to their mum
- not sleep tonight

1 _____

2 _____

3 _____

4 _____

Grammar

18 **Make six questions with should. Write them in your notebook.**

How What Where When	people	go do travel spend time wear use	in your city. for a sore throat. in your city or country. on a rainy day. to weddings. mobile phones.

19 **Use the prompts, or your own ideas, to write suggestions. Use could.**

(travel in your city) → train → cycle → walk

(rainy days) → watch TV → play board games → read books

(in your country) → visit museums → go shopping → see famous places

(sore throat) → drink lemon and honey → suck sweets → see a doctor

(wear to weddings) → men wear suit and tie → women wear pretty dresses → traditional clothes

(mobile phone use) → telephone friends → see the time → check email

1 In my city, *you could take the train, you could cycle or you could walk.*

2 On rainy days, _____

_____

3 In my country, _____

_____

4 When you have a sore throat, _____

_____

5 To weddings, _____

_____

6 With my mobile phone, _____

_____

20 **Read and choose the correct answers**

1 Doctors haven't got a _____ for everything.

   a benefit   **b** cure   **c** home remedy

2 Many doctors tell you to take _____ for a headache.

   a painkillers   **b** vinegar   **c** ingredients

3 Tea is one of the oldest _____.

   a medicines   **b** home remedies **c** illnesses

4 Hot chicken soup has got many health _____.

   a remedies   **b** benefits   **c** cures

76

21 **Listen, read and circle. Then write the correct remedy.**

   Cinnamon   Garlic   Ginger

http://www.remediesrus.com

1 _____ is used around the world as a home remedy for many different problems. For example, many people take it when they've got **¹ a headache / stomachache**. In Japan, when children have got a **² cough / cold**, mothers give them a tea made from it. In Europe, people drink it in hot water with honey and lemon to help a sore throat.

2 _____ is also a common home remedy. In Spain, people add it to their tea to help with colds and coughs. Some Native Americans put it on **³ mosquito / bee** stings. It helps stop the sting from hurting.

3 _____ is another common home remedy. Many people use it for colds, but did you know you can also use it for a **⁴ toothache / backache**? Just mix some with honey and put it on the sore tooth. This not only helps the tooth hurt less but also **⁵ smells / tastes** delicious.

22 **Look at 21 and ✓.**

	bee sting	cold	sore throat	stomachache	toothache
ginger					
garlic					
cinnamon					

23 **Match.**

1 A relaxing drink. Sometimes it's a home remedy for sore throats.

2 When you rub someone to help them relax.

3 Sleep is the best way to do this.

4 When you've got a temperature, this makes your body feel cooler.

5 You feel this before exams or during difficult times.

a herbal tea

b rest

c massage

d stress

e vinegar

TH■NK BIG

These are some common illnesses around the world. Write **HR** when you should use a home remedy or **D** when you should go to the doctor.

allergies ☐   malaria ☐   vomiting ☐   sore throat ☐

headache ☐   muscle pain ☐   cold ☐   cough ☐

high fever ☐   bad cut ☐

Are there any illnesses for which you should do both? Why?

_____

_____

24 **Are commas used correctly? Read and ✓ or ✗.**

> **1 a** First, I eat a healthy breakfast. Then I go swimming.
>
> **b** First I eat a healthy breakfast. Then, I go swimming.
>
> **2 a** You should drink some tea take some medicine and sleep.
>
> **b** You should drink some tea, take some medicine and sleep.
>
> **3 a** I take good care of myself. She takes good care of herself too.
>
> **b** I take good care of myself. She takes good care of herself, too.

25 **Add commas in the correct places.**

1 I get a lot of rest drink water exercise and eat fruit.

2 I don't eat biscuits cake chocolate or sweets.

3 First I should eat a healthy dinner. Then I should do my homework. Finally I should go to bed.

4 The four kinds of germs are bacteria fungi protozoa and viruses.

5 You should drink some tea. You should take some medicine too.

6 First he should take some medicine. After that he should have some soup.

26 **Write answers. Remember to use commas.**

1 I want to eat a healthy lunch. What should I eat?

_____

_____

2 I want to be healthy and exercise. What should I do?

_____

_____

3 I've got stomachache and a fever. What should I do?

_____

_____

27 **Read and circle kn and wr.**

knee   breakfast   wrist

knight   write   wrong

know   knock   right

now   wrap

28 **Underline the words with kn and wr. Then read aloud.**

1 The knight knows how to write.

2 He wraps his knee and knots the rope.

29 **Connect the letters. Then write.**

1 kn   eck   **a** _ _ _ _ _

2 wr   ock   **b** _ _ _ _ _

30 **Listen and write.**

81

What's wrong, ¹_____, wrong?

The ²_____ knocked his

Knee, knee, knee

And his wrist, wrist, ³_____.

I ⁴_____! Wrap his knee

And ⁵_____ his wrist!

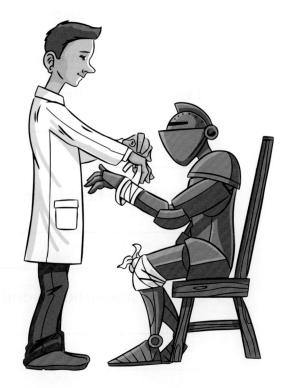

31 Read and match.

1 We have to

2 Germs make

3 Bacteria is

4 Germs get into

a one kind of germ.

b many places.

c protect ourselves from germs.

d a kind of poison called a toxin.

32 Read and circle.

1 She stays up late every night. She should take better care of **himself** / **herself**.

2 They take good care of **themselves** / **ourselves**. They exercise every morning.

3 I eat lots of crisps. I should take better care of **myself** / **yourself**.

4 You always eat a healthy lunch. You take good care of **yourself** / **ourselves**.

33 Look and write. Then complete the sentences with should or shouldn't.

| allergies | cut | fever | headache | sore throat | stomachache |

1 She's got a _____. She _____ drink water and rest.

2 He's got a _____. He _____ talk too much.

3 She's got a _____. She _____ go to school.

4 He's got _____. He _____ eat so many sweets.

5 She's got _____. She _____ go outside.

6 He's got a _____. He _____ take better care of himself.

unit 5

Weird and Wild
Animals

1 **Look and write. Then match.**

| angler fish   coconut crabs   tarsiers   Tasmanian devils   volcano rabbits |

1 _____

a They've got long teeth and they live in oceans all over the world. We don't know how many there are.

2 _____

b They've got big eyes and brown fur. They live in Southeast Asia but we don't know their population.

3 _____

c They've got a population of more than 100,000 and they live on islands in the Pacific Ocean. They're orange and brown.

4 _____

d They've got grey fur and they live on volcanoes in Mexico. They've got a population of between 2,000 and 12,000.

5 _____

e They've got black and white fur. They've got a population of between 10,000 and 25,000 and you can find them in Tasmania.

2 **Listen and write. Then draw.**

♪ **Understanding Animals** 𝄞

Do you know a lot about animals?
How many different kinds there are?
Some are ¹_____ and
Some are ²_____
And some are just bizarre!

Understanding animals is good for us to do
Because learning about animals helps us
And helps them, too!

Some live in ³_____ or in the
⁴_____
And some live where it's hot.
Some are beautiful and some are cute
And some are... well, they're not!

Chorus

It's important to learn about animals,
Though many seem strange, it's true.
Because when we learn about animals,
We learn about ourselves, too.

Chorus

3 **Write the animals.**

big	small	live in trees	live in the sea

Read. Then complete the sentences.

Chimps are Clever!

Christina is watching a TV programme about chimpanzees. She learns that chimps are clever and amazing animals. They can climb trees, talk to other chimps and use tools to get food. But there are not many chimps left in the wild. They are endangered because people are moving into their habitat. Sam can talk, climb trees and use tools to get food, too. He hopes he isn't endangered!

1 Christina is watching a programme about _____ or chimps.

2 Chimps are _____ and amazing animals.

3 They can climb trees and _____ to each other.

4 Chimps use _____ to get food.

5 There aren't many chimps in the wild – they are _____.

5 Answer about you.

1 Can you do any of the things that chimps can do?

_____

2 Do you like chimps? Why/Why not?

_____

THINK BIG **Chimps use tools to get food. What tools do you use to...**

a cook/eat food? _____

b do your homework? _____

c stay clean? _____

6 Listen and stick. Then write.

1

2

3

1990s: more than 100,000

100 years ago: about 100,000

100 years ago: about 90,000

Now: _____

Now: _____

Now: _____

7 Read and complete.

		There were...	There are...
	Komodo dragon	How many? *more than 20,000* When? *fifty years ago*	How many? *fewer than 5,000* When? *now*
	Andean condor	How many? *many* When? *in the past*	How many? *about 10,000* When? *now*
	Tasmanian devil	How many? *100,000* When? *twenty-five years ago*	How many? *between 10,000 and 25,000* When? *now*

1 A: _____ [_____] _____ in the past?

B: _____ many. Now _____ about 10,000.

2 A: _____ [_____] _____ twenty-five years ago?

B: _____ 100,000. Now _____ between 10,000 and 25,000.

3 A: _____ [_____] _____ fifty years ago?

B: _____ more than 20,000. Now _____ fewer than 5,000.

Language in Action

8 **Why are they endangered? Follow each maze and complete the dialogues.**

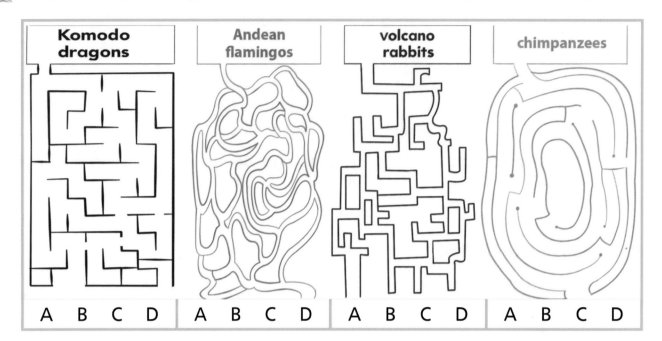

Komodo dragons	Andean flamingos	volcano rabbits	chimpanzees
A B C D	A B C D	A B C D	A B C D

A = Their habitat's polluted.   C = People are moving into their habitat.
B = People are killing them.   D = People are destroying their habitat.

1 **A:** _____ are Komodo dragons endangered?

B: They're endangered _____ [   ].

2 **A:** _____ are Andean flamingos endangered?

B: They're endangered _____ [   ].

3 **A:** _____ are volcano rabbits endangered?

B: They're endangered _____ [   ].

4 **A:** _____ are chimpanzees endangered?

B: They're endangered _____ [   ].

9 **Write the question and answer.**

_____

_____ (coconut crabs)?

_____

_____ (people destroying their habitat).

10 **Read and choose the correct answers.**

1 A _____ hunts and kills animals to eat.

   a predator   **b** trap

2 When there are only a few of one type of animal, they are _____.

   a extinct   **b** endangered

3 People hunt red pandas for their _____.

   a fur   **b** hair

4 Animals aren't safe from diseases or hunting when they live in _____.

   a the world   **b** the wild

11 **Listen, read and complete. Which animals do people keep as pets?**

> bamboo   bumblebee   pandas   predators
> salamander   tortoise   wild

Status: Endangered

1   You can sometimes find [1]_____ bats in caves in the forests of Myanmar and Thailand. However, there are now fewer than 6,000 left in the [2]_____ because farmers burn the trees where they live.

2   Most red [3]_____ live in China and the Himalayas and they eat leaves. They hide in trees covered in red moss so that [4]_____ don't see their beautiful red fur. They're endangered – there are now fewer than 10,000 – because people are destroying the [5]_____ forests.

3   The Egyptian [6]_____ is very small – it's only 10 centimetres long. That makes it the smallest of its kind in the world. Many scientists believe there are only 7,500 left in the wild now because people keep them as pets.

4   The Mexican walking fish lives on land and in water. It's called a fish but it's really a type of [7]_____ with small legs. Unfortunately, this strange fish is almost extinct. It lives in streams and ponds but its habitats are mostly polluted now.

12 Why is each animal endangered? Look at **11**. Then write the names and match.

1 _____   2 _____   3 _____   4 _____

a   b   c   d

13 Complete the sentences.

| caves   extinct   polluted   pond   Scientists |

1 Bumbleebee bats live in _____ because they like the dark.

2 The Mexican walking fish is nearly _____. There are less than 1,000 left.

3 Rivers in towns or cities are often _____. You can't swim in them.

4 _____ try to protect endangered species.

5 There's a large _____ at the end of our garden with small fish and frogs in it.

THINK BIG

Which of these animals are extinct? Circle.

1 tiger / chimpanzee / giant panda / dodo

2 Asian elephant / mountain gorilla / T. rex / blue whale

3 orangutan / bumblebee bat / woolly mammoth / red panda

In what order did these three animals become extinct?

First: _____   Second: _____   Third: _____

14 **Circle.**

1 We **could / couldn't** swim in the sea because there were sharks.

2 Sara had toothache so she **could / couldn't** eat any cake.

3 Katie spoke French so she **could / couldn't** understand everybody in Paris.

4 It rained and we **could / couldn't** have our picnic.

5 Last year, pupils **could / couldn't** wear jeans. It was allowed.

6 In the morning, tourists **could / couldn't** visit the zoo. It was open.

15 **Complete the questions about 14. Then write short answers.**

1 _____ (swim/they) in the sea?   _____

2 _____ (eat/Sara) cake?   _____

3 _____ (speak/Katie) French?   _____

4 _____ (have/they) their picnic?   _____

5 _____ (when/wear/pupils) jeans?   _____

6 _____ (when/visit/tourists) the zoo? _____

16 **Look and write.**

Fifty years ago, people...	✓	✗
the River Thames	swim in	go fishing in
Siberia	hunt tigers in	see many Amur tigers
Mexico City	find walking fish in ponds outside	visit Mayan pyramids

1 Fifty years ago, people _could swim in the River Thames but they couldn't_ _____ .

2 Fifty years ago, _____ _____ .

3 _____ _____ .

Grammar

17 **Circle the correct question words.**

1 **What** / **Where** do red pandas live?

2 **Why** / **Where** are Egyptian tortoises endangered?

3 **What** / **When** can you see Bumblebee bats?

4 **Who** / **What** believes there are less than 10,000 red pandas?

5 **Where** / **What** is happening to forests in Thailand?

18 **Look at 17. Match the answers to the questions.**

a People are cutting down the trees. ☐

b Scientists. ☐

c In bamboo forests. ☐

d Because they're popular pets. ☐

e At night or in the dark. ☐

19 **Find and write questions. Use the words from the box.**

| What   Where   Who   Why |

1 animals/be/endangered/in your country?

_____

2 be/your best friend/at school?

_____

3 go/you/at weekends?

_____

4 learn/you/English?

_____

20 **Look at 19. Write answers for you.**

1 In my country, the grey wolf is endangered. _____

2 _____

3 _____

4 _____

21 **Read and complete.**

| breathe | giants | lizard | mythical | myths | real | scary | wings |

There's only one ¹_____ dragon. It's called the Komodo dragon and it lives on a tiny Indonesian island. Actually, it isn't a dragon, it's a very large ²_____. All other dragons are ³_____ creatures. That means they only exist in ⁴_____ or fairy stories.

Some dragon tales are very frightening – they tell us about ⁵_____ beasts. These beasts are very large – they're ⁶_____ of the sky. They've got enormous ⁷_____ and they ⁸_____ fire.

22 **Listen, read and circle.**

95

1 In North America and Europe, dragons are
- **good / evil**
- **fire-breathing / real**
- **funny / scary**

2 In China, Japan and Korea, dragons are
- beautiful and **magical / evil**
- **fire-breathing / helpful**
- **scary / not scary**

3 In Oceania and Australia, one dragon is
- called a **Western / Bunyip**
- **friendly / scary**
- made of different parts of different **animals / people**

4 In Indonesia, dragons are
- **real / mythical**
- **large lizards / birds**
- **extinct / endangered**

23 **Look at 21 and 22. Read and circle T for true and F for false.**

1 Dragons aren't mythical creatures. T F

2 All dragons can fly. T F

3 In North America and Europe, dragons are evil. T F

4 Dragons in China are made up of different animal parts. T F

5 In Oceania, dragons are scary. T F

6 Dragons are extinct in Indonesia. T F

7 In Japan, dragons are lucky. T F

8 In Indonesia, dragons are large lizards. T F

24 **Find and write four pairs of synonyms and three pairs of antonyms.**

1 tale

a story

2 giant

b frightening

3 humans

c evil

4 good

d south

5 scary

e mythical

6 real

f people

7 north

g very big

Synonyms	Antonyms

THINK BIG **Where can you see examples of dragons or mythical creatures? Think of five places.**

1 _____ 2 _____ 3 _____

4 _____ 5 _____

25 **Look and match.**

1 exclamation mark
2 full stop
3 question mark

26 **Write a full stop, a question mark or an exclamation mark.**

1 How many chimps were there 100 years ago____

2 Coconut crabs live on islands in the Pacific Ocean____

3 Wow____ That frog is so amazing____

4 Why are chimps endangered____

5 Look____ A dragon____

6 They've got a population of 100,000____

27 **Write sentences. Use a full stop, a question mark or an exclamation mark.**

1
angler fish

_____

_____

2
tigers

_____

_____

3
Tasmanian devils

_____

_____

4
volcano rabbits

_____

_____

5
Andean condors

_____

_____

6
black rhinos

_____

_____

28 **Read and circle ph and wh.**

phone   panda   wheel

phantom

photo   white   wild

whale

wheat

dolphin   fish

29 **Underline the words with ph and wh. Then read aloud.**

1   When was the white elephant in the wheat?

2   I took a photo with my phone of a whale and a dolphin.

30 **Connect the letters. Then write.**

1   ph   en   a _ _ _ _

2   wh   one   b _ _ _ _ _

31 **Listen and write.**

The phantom's got a ¹_____

On his ²_____

Of a ³_____ wheel

And some ⁴_____.

32 **Unscramble and complete.**

1 Some scientists believe there are fewer than 7,500 Egyptian tortoises left in the _____. (ldiw)

2 Most bumblebee bats live in _____ in Thailand. (vesac)

3 Red pandas eat _____ leaves. (ooambb)

4 Most scientists believe that the Mexican walking fish is almost _____. (cnetxit)

33 **Complete the dialogues with words from the box.**

because	chimpanzees	habitat	how many
tarsiers	there are	there were	

1

A: Why are _____ endangered?

B: They're endangered _____ people are destroying their _____.

2

A: _____ Andean condors are there now?

B: _____ only about 10,000 left in the wild.

3

A: How many _____ were there a hundred years ago?

B: _____ more than a million.

34 **Read and write could or couldn't.**

A: We ¹_____ touch the Komodo dragons. They're too dangerous. People ²_____ only look at them from far away.

B: ³_____ you watch them eat?

A: Yes. They ⁴_____ fit a small deer in their mouth. It was amazing!

unit 6

Life Long Ago

1 **Read and write the letters. Then trace the path.**

L travel by car

I travelled by horse and carriage

G had oil lamps

E listened to the radio

N cook in a microwave

O washed clothes by hand

L wash clothes in a washing machine

G cooked on a coal stove

A have electric lights

F listen to an mp3 player

O have a mobile phone

! used a phone with an operator

2 **Look at the letters in 1. Follow the path and write the letters. What do they spell?**

____ ____ ____ ____ ____ ____ ____ ____ ____ ____ ____ ____ ____

3 Listen and match.

In the Old Days

a

Now there's water from the tap.

c

Now there are computers.

e

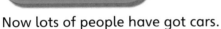

Now lots of people have got cars.

Life one hundred years ago
Was different, you see.
¹ There were no computers
² And there was no TV.

**Life was different in the old days.
Life was different in so many ways.**

³ Children used to get water
From pumps or wells outdoors.
Now we just turn on the tap
And out fresh water pours!

Chorus

Life was so much slower!
⁴ Few people had a car.
⁵ Children used to walk to school
And they walked very far!

Chorus

b

Now there's TV.

d

Now children take a school bus.

4 Write about now and long ago.

Now

Long Ago

_____   _____
_____   _____
_____   _____
_____   _____
_____   _____
_____   _____

5 **Read. Then circle T for true and F for false.**

Life was Nicer Then

Sam and his grandma are watching the TV. Sam wants to change the channel but he's too lazy to get the TV remote control. They didn't have remote controls when Sam's grandma was a child. They used to walk to the TV to change the channel. They only had three channels when Grandma was young and she thinks life was nicer then.

The microwave beeps. Grandma sometimes uses a microwave to make dinner. Maybe some things about modern life are nicer!

1	Grandma is too lazy to change the channel.	**T**	**F**
2	People didn't watch TV when Sam's grandma was young.	**T**	**F**
3	There were no remote controls when Sam's grandma was a child.	**T**	**F**
4	There are only three channels now.	**T**	**F**
5	Grandma uses a microwave to cook.	**T**	**F**

THINK BIG

What did your grandma have when she was a child? Read and ✓ or ✗. Then write.

computer ☐ phone ☐ washing machine ☐ microwave ☐

car ☐ bike ☐ TV remote control ☐ books ☐ radio ☐

My grandma had _____

_____.

She didn't have _____

_____.

6 Listen and stick. Number in order.

a  ☐

b  ☐

c  ☐

d  ☐

7 Read and write the answers. Use **did** or **didn't**.

1 A: Did your grandmother have a TV when she was young?

B: _____

2 A: Did people have cars fifty years ago?

B: _____

3 A: Did your grandfather play video games when he was a child?

B: _____

4 A: Did people have washing machines 200 hundred years ago?

B: _____

8 Complete the questions and answers.

1

A: _____ mum _____ a mobile phone at school?

B: _____, _____. She used public phones.

2

A: _____ dad _____ a computer at school?

B: _____, _____. It was big and slow.

9 **Complete the sentences.**

1 **A:** Before computers, how _____
keep in touch?

B: They _____.

2 **A:** Before washing machines, how _____
wash clothes?

B: They _____.

3 **A:** Before electricity, what _____
for light?

B: They _____.

4 **A:** Before cars, what _____
for transportation?

B: They _____.

10 **Answer about you.**

1 When she was young, what did your grandma use to do at night?

_____

2 When you were six, how did you use to go to school?

_____

11 **Look in your house. What used to be different?**

1 _____

_____

2 _____

_____

3 _____

_____

12 **Complete the sentences.**

| average speed | distance | engine | multiply | number of | per hour |

1 The _____ of a modern plane is about 885 km per hour.

2 Planes are a great way to travel a long _____ because they're fast.

3 The average man can walk at a speed of 5 km _____.

4 Bad traffic means there is a large _____ cars on the roads.

5 If you _____ ten by ten, it makes a hundred.

6 A car can't travel without an _____.

13 **Listen, read and circle. How did people travel before cars?**

1   What did people do before they had cars? Well, lucky people used to travel by horse and carriage. And unlucky people walked. Both forms of travel were **¹ uncomfortable / slow** but the horse and carriage was a bit more comfortable. It had an average speed of 8 kilometres (km) per hour. Historians believe people didn't travel for longer than about three hours a day, probably because it was very **² tiring / expensive**.

Horse and Carriage

Model T

2   Mr Henry Ford built the first Model T, or 'Tin Lizzie', in 1908. It changed the way we travel. For the first time, a car wasn't a luxury. The car became a **³ popular / cheap** means of transport and everybody with a job and some money could buy one. The Model T had an average speed of 40 km per hour. Suddenly, there were more vehicles on the roads and it was more **⁴ exciting / dangerous**.

3   Today, there are many different **⁵ modern / new** cars. Some are for racing, some are luxury cars and some are family cars. They're all faster than they used to be. An average family car can travel at a speed of more than 150 km per hour. But they never do. The average speed of modern cars is 90 km per hour. This is because there are strict speed limits and there is lots of **⁶ noise / traffic**.

Modern Car

14 Look at 13. Read and answer.

1 How many hours did people travel each day with a horse and carriage?

_____

2 Who could buy a Model T? _____

3 Today, cars can't travel fast. Why not?

_____

15 Look at the average speeds in 13 and solve the equations.

1 A horse and carriage travels for 10 hours. How far does it travel?

_____ x _____ = _____ km

average   number   distance
speed   of hours   travelled

2 A Model T travels for 6 hours. How far does it travel?

_____ x _____ = _____ km

3 A horse and carriage travels for 8 hours. How far does it travel?

_____ x _____ = _____ km

4 A modern car travels for 2 hours. How far does it travel?

_____ x _____ = _____ km

5 A Model T travels for 7 hours. How far does it travel?

_____ x _____ = _____ km

6 A modern car travels for 3 hours. How far does it travel?

_____ x _____ = _____ km

THINK BIG

Look at 15 and cross out the answers. Then use the other numbers to make a new equation.

3   40   64   80   120   180   240   270   280

A Model T travels for _____ hours. How far does it travel?

_____ x _____ = _____ km

16 **What were these people doing yesterday? Complete.**

1 At eight o'clock, The Graham family _____were swimming_____ (swim) in a lake.

2 At nine o'clock, Mrs Cross _____ (put) clothes in her washing machine.

3 At ten o'clock, Harry's dog _____ (eat) an old shoe.

4 At eleven o'clock, Jordan's sister _____ (look) out of the car window. She _____ (feel) very bored.

5 At twelve o'clock, the Gray twins _____ (watch) their favourite DVD.

6 At two o'clock, the neighbours _____ (have) a party in their garden.

17 **Look and write.**

1 8 a.m. – Dad
wait for the bus ✓
drive ✗

_At 8 a.m., Dad was waiting for the bus. He wasn't driving._____

2 12 p.m. – dog
bark loudly ✗
go for a walk ✓

_____

3 6 p.m. – Mum
cook dinner ✗
have pizza with friends ✓

_____

4 7 p.m. – Eli
play computer games ✓
do homework ✗

_____

5 8 p.m. – Sofia
watch TV ✗
study ✓

_____

6 11 a.m. – Dad
sleep ✗
run ✓

_____

18 **Write questions.**

1 what/you/do/at 10 p.m./last night?

_____

2 you/watch TV/at 8 a.m./yesterday morning?

_____

3 you/have/breakfast/at 9 a.m.?

_____

4 where/you/go/after school/yesterday afternoon?

_____

5 your family/eat/dinner/at 8 p.m./last night?

_____

19 **Look at 18. Answer the questions for you.**

1 _____

2 _____

3 _____

4 _____

5 _____

20 **Complete the sentences.**

> had   only goes   used to go   was feeling   was racing
> was travelling   were driving   were enjoying

When Carlos was young, he [1]_____ on holiday with his family every year. Now he [2]_____ with his friends! One August, they [3]_____ through France for their summer holiday. Dad [4]_____ a brand new car. Carlos' parents [5]_____ themselves but Carlos [6]_____ bored. The car [7]_____ at an average speed of 90 km per hour – so fast that Carlos couldn't see anything. Carlos asked for a bike.

That summer, Carlos' parents drove and Carlos cycled. Five years later, Carlos [8]_____ his bicycle in the Tour de France competition!

21 **Read and circle.**

1 When you haven't got **technology** / **running water**, it's difficult to keep the house clean.

2 Your **tribe** / **nomad** are the people you live with. They're like a big family.

3 If your house hasn't got **heating** / **electricity**, you can't use a computer or a TV.

4 **Traditional** / **Cultural** habits are old habits from the past.

5 Mobile phones, computers and TVs all use modern **electricity** / **technology**.

114
22 **Listen, read and write. Which tribe changes home quite often?**

| ancestors | forests | language | nomadic | reindeer | tundra |

The Hmong

1 The Hmong are hill people. They live in the mountains of Southeast Asia. They've got their own way of life and their own ¹_____. You won't find much modern technology in a traditional Hmong village, because people there live the way their ²_____ did, 2,000 years ago.

The Maasai

2 The Maasai of Kenya are a ³_____ tribe. This means they move from place to place and make new homes each time. They often live in ⁴_____ and build their homes out of things they can find in nature. Their villages haven't got running water or electricity, so they can't use modern technology in their homes.

The Koryak

3 The Koryak live in the northern part of Russia's Pacific coast. Their land is Arctic ⁵_____ and it's very cold. For food, they herd ⁶_____ and catch fish. Koryak children haven't got time for playing computer games or surfing the Internet because they hunt for food with their parents. They also make some of their clothes. They wear warm hats made of reindeer skins to protect them from the freezing temperatures.

23 **Look at 22 and ✓.**

	The Hmong	The Koryak	The Maasai
1 live in Russia			
2 move from place to place			
3 live in Southeast Asia			
4 wear reindeer skin hats			
5 live in Kenya			
6 live like people did 2,000 years ago			

24 **Look at 22. Choose words from the box to match the definitions.**

1 People from your family or tribe who aren't alive. _____

2 We use this to speak and communicate. _____

3 These people don't stay in one place. _____

4 It's a dry and cold place and there aren't many trees. _____

5 A large animal that likes the cold weather. _____

Which of these things are most difficult?
Number 1 (not very difficult) to 5 (very difficult).

THINK BIG

building your own house ☐

changing house every few years ☐

looking for water to drink ☐

living in the mountains ☐

living without electricity ☐

looking for food ☐

living in a very cold place ☐

Which tribe do you think lives the most difficult life? Why?

_____

_____

Put speech marks in the correct places.

1 Did they watch films in the 1920s? he asked.

2 I used to play football, said John.

3 Jamie yelled, I got a new bike!

4 Karen said, I wrote a letter last night.

 Rewrite the sentences. Use said or asked and speech marks.

How did people travel in 1905?

Did you use to ride in a horse and carriage?

They used to ride in a horse and carriage.

I'm not that old!

Ed   Mum

1 _____

2 _____

3 _____

4 _____

Look and write what they are saying. Use said, asked or yelled and speech marks.

1

2

28 **Read and circle ge and dge.**

fridge   cage   watched
traditional   washed   large
badge   edge
bridge   page   age

29 **Underline the words with ge and dge. Then read aloud.**

1 Look over the edge of the hedge. There's a bridge.

2 The boy's wearing a large badge and carrying a cage.

30 **Connect the letters. Then write.**

1 ca   dge   **a** _ _ _ _

2 ba   ge   **b** _ _ _ _ _

3 lar   ge   **c** _ _ _ _

4 e   dge   **d** _ _ _ _ _

 **31** **Listen and write.**

There's a ¹_____ fridge
On the ²_____.
There's a large ³_____
In the ⁴_____.

32 **Read and solve the equations.**

1 A school bus has an average speed of 60 kilometres per hour. How far does it travel in 3 hours?

_____ x _____ = _____ km

2 A bike has an average speed of 20 kilometres per hour. How far does it travel in 6 hours?

_____ x _____ = _____ km

33 **Circle and write.**

1 **A: Did / Do** people have microwaves 100 years ago?

B: _____

2 **A:** Did your city or town **had / have** cars ten years ago?

B: _____

3 **A:** Did people **use to / used to** listen to mp3 players before electricity?

B: _____

4 **A:** Did your dad **travel / travelled** to school by horse and carriage?

B: _____

34 **Circle four things that didn't exist long ago. Write sentences with didn't use to in your notebook.**

35 **What were you and you family doing at these times yesterday?**

Eight o' clock in the morning _____

One o' clock lunchtime _____

Seven o' clock in the evening _____

Sue's Path

1. **Look at Units 4, 5 and 6. Choose words from the units. Write them in the charts.**

2. **Draw one path. Gather information and add your own.**

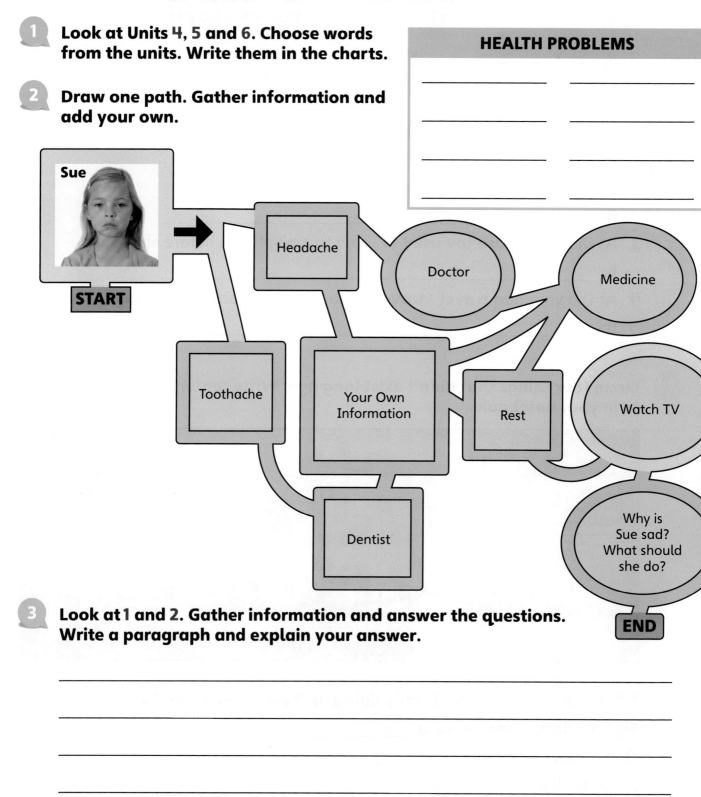

HEALTH PROBLEMS	
_____	_____
_____	_____
_____	_____
_____	_____

3. **Look at 1 and 2. Gather information and answer the questions. Write a paragraph and explain your answer.**

_____

_____

_____

_____

ENDANGERED ANIMALS

_____

_____

_____

_____

TECHNOLOGY NOW

_____

_____

_____

_____

END

Endangered Animals

TIGERS: Used to be 100,000. Fewer than 3,200!

KOMODO DRAGON: Used to be 20,000. Fewer than 5,000!

Why are they endangered? What should we do?

END

Long Ago and Now

Your Own Information

What did people use? What do they use now?

unit 7 Special Days

1 **Look and write the special days.**

1 _____

2 _____

3 _____

4 _____

5 _____

6 _____

2 **Read and circle T for true and F for false.**

1 My parents' anniversary is celebrated by my mum and dad.   **T**   **F**

2 New Year's Day is before New Year's Eve.   **T**   **F**

3 School Sports Day is for parents, not children.   **T**   **F**

4 My dad celebrates Father's Day.   **T**   **F**

3 **Listen and write. Use the words from the box.**

What Do We Do on Special Days?

This ¹_____ is a special day –
The last day of the year.
We're ²_____ stay up very late.
At midnight we're going to cheer!

Special days are cool. Special days are fun.
Special days bring special treats for everyone!

On the first of ³_____,
We are going to say,
"Happy New Year!" to everyone
Because it's ⁴_____.

Chorus

There are lots of special days
And this one is a treat.
We're going to
Have ⁵_____
And ⁶_____
And delicious food to eat!

Chorus

fireworks
Friday
going to
January
New Year's Day
parades

4 **Look at 3 and ✓ the correct answers.**

1 This Friday is…

☐ 30ᵗʰ December. ☐ 31ˢᵗ December. ☐ 1ˢᵗ January.

2 They are going to cheer…

☐ at lunchtime. ☐ in the afternoon. ☐ at midnight.

3 On New Year's Eve they…

☐ stay up late. ☐ go to bed early. ☐ sleep late.

5 **Read. Then answer the questions.**

The Anniversary Party

Sam knows his parents' wedding anniversary is the 10th. He's planning a big celebration for their anniversary on 10th June. They're going to go out for a special dinner. Sam is making a cake. His parents like the plans but there's a problem. Their anniversary is on 10th July, not 10th June!

1 Why is Sam planning a celebration? _____

2 Where are they going to go? _____

3 What's the problem? _____

6 **Write about you and your family.**

1 My birthday is on _____.

2 My mum's birthday is on _____.

3 My dad's birthday is on _____.

4 My parents' wedding anniversary is on _____.

THINK BIG

Think and write. What do you think Sam's parents are going to say next?

_____
_____

_____
_____

131

7 Listen and stick. Then listen and write the special day and what they are going to do.

1

2

3

_____

_____

_____

_____

_____

_____

8 Answer the questions about Sarah's calendar.

Sun	Mon	Tue	Wed	Thu	Fri	Sat
1	2	3 Today	4	5	6	7 Birthday party
8	9	10	11 Parents' anniversary	12	13	14 Sister visits friend
15	16	17	18 Watch parade	19	20	21 Watch fireworks

1 When is Sarah going to have her birthday party? _____

_____

2 When are her parents going to celebrate their anniversary? _____

_____

3 When is her sister going to visit her friend? _____

_____

4 Is she going to watch the parade on the 17th? _____

5 Are they going to watch the fireworks on Saturday? _____

9 **Listen and match.**

			JUNE			
SUNDAY	MONDAY	TUESDAY	WEDNESDAY	THURSDAY	FRIDAY	SATURDAY
					1	2
3	4	5	6	7	8	9
10	11	12	13	14	15	16
17	18	19	20	21	22	23
24	25	26	27	28	29	30

Mum's birthday

sports day

Father's Day

watch a parade

Grandparents' anniversary

Midsummer's Day

10 **Read and cross out the letters. Then write the special days.**

1 Cross out the first, third, fifth, ninth, tenth, twelfth and fourteenth letters.

G E T A B R T H L N D O A M Y

— — — — —   — — —

2 Cross out the first, third, seventh, tenth, thirteenth, sixteenth, seventeenth and twentieth letters.

B M O I D S R U M H M E P R S Y N D A O Y

— — — — — — — — —'— — — — —

3 Cross out the second, fourth, sixth, seventh, ninth, eleventh, sixteenth, seventeenth and nineteenth letters.

N A E H W P V Y I E N A R S D E V A E Y

— — — — — — — — —'— — — — —

11 **Complete the sentences.**

> attraction   clean   fight   takes place   torches

1 Every year in Buñol there's a big tomato _____. ☐

2 In one festival in Thailand, people carry _____ of fire down from the mountain. ☐

3 The Monkey Buffet festival in Thailand isn't a popular tourist _____. ☐

4 It's very unusual to leave the Holi festival with _____ clothes on. ☐

5 Quyllur Rit'i only _____ in June. ☐

136
12 **Listen, read and circle. Are the sentences in 11 correct? Put a ✓ or a ✗.**

Holi, The Festival of Colours

1   This festival takes place every year to **¹ watch / celebrate** the end of winter and the arrival of spring. It's celebrated in India, Nepal and other places. It's probably the most colourful festival in the whole world. During Holi, people throw water and coloured **² paper / powder**. People like to wear white clothes to Holi and watch them stain with all the different colours.

Tomatina, The Tomato Festival

2   Every year, on the last Wednesday of August, there's a **³ clean / messy** festival in Buñol, Spain, where people throw tomatoes at each other. The festival started in 1945. There was no real reason for it. It was just good fun.

The Monkey Buffet

3   On the last weekend in November, the people of Lopburi, Thailand, invite hundreds of monkeys to a **⁴ feast / fight** of peanuts, fruit and vegetables. People come from all over the world to watch the monkeys eat.

Quyllur Rit'i, The Festival of the Snow Star

4   It takes place every May or June on a **⁵ volcano / glacier** in Peru. People celebrate with music and dancing for three days and nights. The festival finishes with everyone leaving carrying fire torches.

13 **Look at 12. Circle T for true and F for false.**

1 The Festival of Colours takes place in China. T F

2 People usually wear white clothes to Holi. T F

3 The Tomato Festival is celebrated in Spain. T F

4 People celebrate it to say thank you for all the tomatoes. T F

5 The Monkey Buffet takes place at the end of November in Thailand. T F

6 People celebrate the Festival of the Snow Star for three weeks in Peru. T F

14 **Answer the questions.**

1 Who are the guests at the Monkey Buffet?

_____

2 What makes the streets messy at the tomato festival?

_____

3 Why is it icy cold at the festival of the Snow Star?

_____

4 Why does the coloured powder stick to clothes at Holi?

_____

Think and write. What are you going to take with you?

THINK BIG

You're going to The Tomato Festival.

_____

You're going to the Festival of the Snow Star.

_____

15 **Read and choose the correct answers.**

1 Sara _____ a new dress yesterday because she's going to a wedding on Saturday.

   a bought   **b** is buying

2 Damian took his violin to school because he _____ in the school concert later.

   a played   **b** is going to play

3 We watched a programme about animals in the wild because we _____ a project next week at school.

   a did   **b** are doing

4 Mum _____ Dad a cake this afternoon because it's his fortieth birthday tomorrow.

   a baking   **b** baked

5 Dad _____ some more petrol in the car last night because we're going on a long journey.

   a puts   **b** put

6 I gave my old phone to my little sister because I'm _____ a new one!

   a going to get   **b** get

16 **Complete the sentences. Use the correct form of the verb.**

1 Tim _____ (not study) last night because he's going to do revision today.

2 Gail wasn't at the party because she _____ (go) on holiday with her family tomorrow.

3 Marie _____ (not meet) her friend yesterday because she was busy.

4 They woke up very early because they're _____ (climb) a mountain today.

5 We didn't bring our swimming costumes because we _____ (not swim) today.

6 I finished my homework quickly today because I _____ (watch) a DVD with my best friend.

17 **Match. Then write sentences. Use going to.**

1 Dad/buy/a new camera

2 We/decorate/our classroom

3 Mum/buy/presents

4 Kim/learn/all about computers

5 Tom/stay/at home

6 Jenny/eat/a big dinner

because

a run in a race tomorrow.

b take photos of the Monkey Buffet.

c get a new laptop.

d watch his favourite TV programme.

e meet our American cousins.

f have visitors from a school abroad.

1 _____

2 _____

3 _____

4 _____

5 _____

6 _____

18 **Complete the sentences for you.**

1 _____ because I'm going to meet a friend after school this afternoon.

2 I went to bed early because _____.

3 My mum bought me some new clothes _____.

4 _____ because I'm going to go on holiday with my friend's family.

19 **Read and choose the correct answers.**

1 What don't you see on a calendar?

    a dates   **b** numbers   **c** days   **d** planets

2 Which one is a superstition?

    a I usually eat chicken on Mondays.

    b I always buy birthday presents for friends.

    c I wouldn't marry in a leap year.

3 When you propose you usually…

    a invite someone to your party.

    b borrow some money.

    c ask someone to marry you.

20 139

Listen, read and write the numbers. Which day is the leap day?

| 49 | 366 | 2008 | 1 | 29 | 365 |

1   We usually say a year is ¹_____ days long because that's about the time it takes Earth to travel around the Sun. It actually takes 365 days, 5 hours, ²_____ minutes and 12 seconds. The extra 5 hours, 49 minutes and 12 seconds add up to an extra day every four years – on ³_____th February. This day is called leap day. Years with the extra day are called leap years. These years have always got ⁴_____ days. We know when there's a leap year because these years can be divided evenly by four. For example, 2004, ⁵_____ and 2012 were leap years.

2   The leap year was put on the calendar only in the ⁶_____st century BC. In ancient times, people were very superstitious about them.

3   In modern times, it's a tradition in many countries for women to propose to their boyfriends on a leap day. Traditionally, men propose to women. But not on leap days! On a leap day, if the woman proposes but the man says 'no', he must buy the woman a present.

4   The only really unlucky people are the ones with birthdays on a leap day. This means their birthday comes only once every four years!

21 **Look at 20. Answer the questions.**

1 How long does it take Earth to travel around the Sun?

_____ days

_____ hours

_____ minutes

_____ seconds

2 How many days are there in a leap year? _____

22 **Solve these problems.**

1 Billy was born on 29ᵗʰ February, 2000. Write the next four years he can celebrate his birthday on 29ᵗʰ February.

_____ _____ _____ _____

2 It's 29ᵗʰ February, 2012. It's Jessi's birthday. Write the next four years she can celebrate her birthday on 29ᵗʰ February.

_____ _____ _____ _____

23 **Read and complete.**

Greece   leap years   unlucky

    Julius Caesar created ¹_____ in the 1ˢᵗ century BC. Greeks and Romans were very superstitious about this year. They thought it was ²_____ to start a journey, start a new job, marry or buy or sell something in a leap year. In ³_____, some people still think it's very unlucky to marry in a leap year.

THINK BIG

What do people believe about leap years in your country? Are they good or bad?

_____

Write a common superstition in your country.

_____

24 **Look and complete the email. Use the words from the box.**

FROM	¹ _____
TO	alex@bigenglish.com
SUBJECT	² _____

Dear
Next weekend
simon@bigenglish.com
Your friend,

³ _____ Alex,

Guess what! It's our street carnival next weekend. There are loads of things planned. I'm going to watch the parade because my sister's in it. She's going to wear special traditional clothes. Then I'm going to buy a present for my grandparents. It's their anniversary on 13ᵗʰ June.

I've got to go. Write back soon!

⁴ _____

Simon

25 **Write an email to a friend. Invite your friend to a celebration.**

Midsummer's Day party   New Year's Day

FROM	
TO	
SUBJECT	

26 **Read and circle ue, u_e and ure.**

cute   glue   bridge

sponge   edge   picture

blue   cube

true   treasure

27 **Underline the words with ue, u_e and ure. Then read aloud.**

1 This is a huge bottle of glue.

2 I drink pure water.

28 **Connect the letters. Then write.**

1 bl   ure   **a** _ _ _ _ _ _

2 c   ue   **b** _ _ _ _

3 nat   ube   **c** _ _ _ _

 29 **Listen and write.**

144

Hi, ¹ _____

Is it ² _____?

It's so ³ _____,

It's so ⁴ _____,

It's really ⁵ _____!

Is that a monster

In the ⁶ _____?

30 **Read and answer.**

Sam's going to the dentist on the ninth of March. On the fifteenth of March, he's going to visit his aunt and uncle. His cousins are on holiday so on the twentieth of March, he's going to visit them. They're going to go to the cinema together.

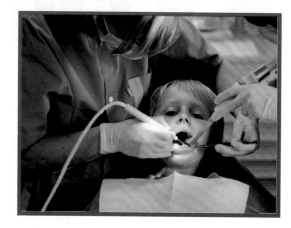

1 Where is Sam going on 9th March? _____

2 What is he going to do on 15th March? _____

3 Is he going to see his cousins on 15th? _____

4 Is he going to see his cousins on 20th? _____

31 **Read and match.**

1 give a   **a** clothes

2 have a   **b** a present

3 watch a   **c** parade

4 watch   **d** party

5 wear different   **e** card

6 get   **f** fireworks

32 **Read and write. Use the words from the box.**

During   For   last   takes place

1 The Festival of Colours _____ every year in India.

2 _____ three days and nights people celebrate with music.

3 The Tomato Festival is on the _____ Wednesday of August.

4 _____ the Monkey Buffet festival, monkeys feast on fruit and vegetables.

unit 8 Hobbies

1 **Draw the path. Connect the pictures. Then complete the question and answer.**

football player → painter → toy car collection → chess player →

coin collection → singer → video game player → shell collection →

doll collection → dancer → basketball player → writer

What _____?

_____

2 **Listen and circle. Then answer the questions.**

The Best and the Worst

Matthew collects toy cars.
He's got one hundred and seven.
But Pam's **car / shell** collection is bigger
She's got three hundred and
Eleven / ten!

Kay is good at games.
She's really good at **music / chess**.
But Paul is even better than Kay.
And Liz, well, she's the best!

What's your hobby, Bobby?
What do you like doing?
What's your hobby, Bobby?
What is fun for you?

Steve is a **great / terrible** singer.
Emma's worse than Steve.
But David's singing is the worst.
When he sings, people leave!

It's **bad / good** to have a hobby.
Some people have got a few.
Even if you're not the best,
It still is fun to do!

Chorus

1 Who collects toy cars? _____

2 How many cars has Matthew got? _____

3 How many cars has Pam got? _____

4 Who is the best at games? _____

5 Is Steve a good singer? _____

6 Do people like listening to David's singing? _____

3 **Read. Then circle T for true and F for false.**

The School Play

Christina's dad is excited about this year's school play. The play is *Snow White*. He wants Christina to be a star in the play. He wants her to be an important character, like Snow White or the Evil Queen. Christina hasn't got those parts. Her friends Lizzie and Ruth have got those parts because they're better singers and actors than Christina. But Christina's the tallest girl in the class, so she's going to be a tree. It's a small part but Christina's dad is very proud of her.

1	Christina's dad thinks the school play is boring.	**T**	**F**
2	He wants Christina to be Snow White.	**T**	**F**
3	Christina is a better singer than Lizzie.	**T**	**F**
4	Christina is taller than all the other girls.	**T**	**F**
5	Christina's going to be a tree.	**T**	**F**

4 **Write about you.**

1 What character would you like to be in *Snow White*? Why?

_____

2 What are you good at?

_____

THINK BIG **Think about Snow White and the Evil Queen. Who do you like better? Why? Use the words from the box.**

friendly
kind nice
old pretty

_____

5 Listen and stick. Then number and write. Use the words from the box.

> the best   the coolest   the worst

a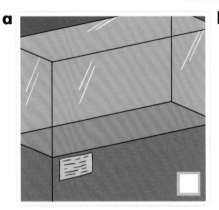

b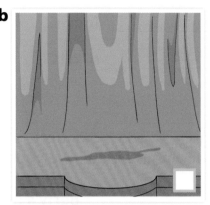

c

_____   _____   _____

6 Complete the table. Use the words from the box.

> bad   better   the best   the worst

☹		worse		good			☺

7 Read and circle the correct words. Then match.

1 Susan's team is **good / better** at basketball. ☐

2 Cassie's story is the **longer / longest** story. ☐

3 Grandpa used to be the **good / best** painter in the city. ☐

4 Diane is worse **than / of** Claire at video games. ☐

5 Jason has a **better / good** shell collection than Craig. ☐

6 This is the **oldest / older** doll in my collection. ☐

a

b

c

d

e

f

8 **Read. Then use a form of big or old to complete each sentence.**

> Philip's got two brothers and three sisters. Pablo's got three brothers and four sisters. Tony's got two brothers and two sisters.

1 Philip's family is _____ Tony's.

2 Pablo's family is _____ of all.

3 Tony's family is _____ .

> Dean's grandma is eighty-six years old. Betty's grandma is seventy-four years old. Harriet's grandma is ninety-one years old.

4 Dean's grandma is _____ Betty's grandma.

5 Betty's grandma is _____ .

6 Harriet's grandma is _____ of all.

9 **Read and answer for you.**

1 What are you good at?

_____

2 What is your mum or dad good at?

_____

3 What is your brother or sister good at?

_____

4 What are you bad at?

_____

5 What is your best friend bad at?

_____

6 What is your cousin bad at?

_____

10 **Number the photos.**

> **1** butterfly collection   **2** doll   **3** embroidery   **4** football

a    b   c    d

156

11 **Listen, read and circle six mistakes. Then write the correct words.**

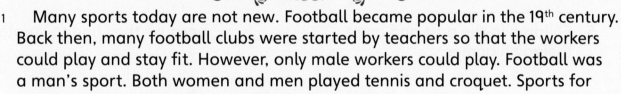

> china   drawing   employers   rocking   skirts   thread

1   Many sports today are not new. Football became popular in the 19th century. Back then, many football clubs were started by teachers so that the workers could play and stay fit. However, only male workers could play. Football was a man's sport. Both women and men played tennis and croquet. Sports for women weren't easy because they had to wear long trousers.

¹ _____   ² _____

2   Girls used to spend a lot of time at home. They did quiet activities with their hands. Many girls liked doing embroidery with a needle and rope. They used to embroider cushions and tablecloths. They also created beautiful pictures of flowers and birds with tiny coloured stitches. ³ _____

3   In the 19th century, the choice of toys for girls and boys was much smaller. Girls used to play with dolls and dolls' houses. They had to be careful because the dolls were made of plastic. They could break quite easily. Jumping horses were also popular with boys and girls. Boys used to play with toy trains and railways. ⁴ _____   ⁵ _____

4   People in the 19th century loved nature. One popular hobby was collecting and playing with butterflies. They caught the butterflies in nets, then pinned them on boards to show their beautiful colours. ⁶ _____

12 **Look at 11. Read and circle.**

In the 19th century,

1 many men played football **in the park / at work**.

2 women used to play **with trains / croquet**.

3 women **went out / stayed at home** a lot.

4 girls' dolls **didn't break / broke** easily.

5 people **set free / showed** the insects they caught.

13 **Complete the sentences.**

> handmade   imagination   net   sewing   spare time

1 You use a needle and thread to do _____.

2 Most people do their hobbies in their _____.

3 These sweets aren't from a shop or a factory. They're _____.

4 Butterflies move quite slowly so it's easy to catch them with a _____.

5 Children in the past had more _____ because they had to create their own games.

Think and write.

THINK BIG

> collecting butterflies   dolls   embroidery   football
> marbles   rocking horse   tennis   trains   TV   video games

19th century   21st century

14 **Read and choose the correct answers.**

1 Butterfly collecting is a _____ than stamp collecting.

  a more interesting   **b** more interesting hobby

2 Football is _____ tennis.

  a more popular than   **b** popular than

3 Embroidery is _____ activity than sewing.

  a a more difficult   **b** more difficult

4 Rats are _____ pets for children.

  a best   **b** the best

5 The British Museum is probably one of _____ museums in London.

  a more interesting   **b** the most interesting

6 Girls are usually _____ than boys.

  a organised   **b** more organised

15 **Do you agree or disagree with the statements in 14? Write your comments. Use more, the most and than.**

1 _____

2 _____

3 _____

4 _____

5 _____

6 _____

16 **Read and complete.**

Did you know that...

1 Robert Downey Jr is one of the _____ (rich) actors in Hollywood?

2 Mawsynram in India has _____ (wet) weather than the UK?

3 some of the _____ (tall) buildings in the world are in Dubai?

4 scientists believe dolphins are _____ (intelligent) than rats or monkeys?

5 raw vegetables are _____ (healthy) than cooked vegetables?

6 with over 8.5 million visitors, the Louvre in Paris is the _____ (popular) museum in the world?

17 **Read and compare.**

funny – *Despicable Me/Shrek/Ice Age*

creative – painting/stamp collecting/sewing

dangerous – skiing/mountain climbing/skydiving

small – Egyptian tortoise/coconut crab/bumblebee bat

hot – Greece/France/Saudi Arabia

tasty – chocolate/cheese/vegetables

1 *Ice Age is funnier than Despicable Me but Shrek is the funniest of all.*

2 _____

3 _____

4 _____

5 _____

6 _____

18 **Write questions. Then answer for you.**

> **Your school:**
> **1** Who is/old pupil/in your class?
> **2** Is/English/popular/other subjects?
> **3** What is/interesting lesson/at school?
> **4** Which sport/exciting/at school?
> **5** Are/lessons/good/homework?

1 _____ _____

2 _____ _____

3 _____ _____

4 _____ _____

5 _____ _____

19 **Make phrases. Then complete the museum information.**

1 underwater   sightings

2 UFO   sculptures

3 locks of   hair

a

b

c

> Come in and leave your _____ !

> Come and find out about _____ !

> Don't miss our _____ !

20 **Listen, read and complete. When did a UFO land in Roswell?**

> artists   experts   landed   marine   potter

1   This museum is in a national ¹_____ park. It's got 400 wonderful sculptures. However, if you want to visit this place, you've got to swim there. Jason DeCaires Taylor, one of the ²_____, wanted his work to be part of the sea life of the Mexican Yucatán Peninsula. You can see it displayed among plants, corals and other marine life. Don't forget your swimming trunks or swimming costume.

2   Roswell, New Mexico, is famous for a UFO sighting in 1947. Many people believe a UFO actually ³_____ there. At Roswell's International UFO Museum and Research Center, you can't actually see any UFOs but you can read the stories people tell about UFOs. The museum holds a festival every year. Many UFO ⁴_____ come to speak at the festival.

3   This museum has got pieces of hair. Each one has a person's name and the date it was cut. The hair is displayed in a cave in Turkey. The museum was started by a ⁵_____, who displayed a single lock of hair in his pottery shop. When he told people the story behind it, they wanted to leave their hair, too – and so the museum's life began.

21 **Look at 20. Write UFO, Hair or Underwater museum.**

1 There's only information here. _____

2 The things you see are part of nature. _____

3 They hold a festival each year. _____

4 It's in a protected area. _____

5 You see hair from different people here. _____

6 It belongs to one man. _____

22 **Read and match.**

1 A person who makes cups and plates.

2 It describes sea life.

3 A person who knows everything about a subject.

4 The rocky homes of tiny underwater animals – they're usually colourful.

5 Looking at things under the water with a mask and breathing tube.

a corals

b snorkelling

c potter

d marine

e expert

Think of your own weird collection for a museum. Draw and then describe it.

THINK
BIG

_____

_____

_____

_____

_____

_____

23 **Look and complete the informal letter. Use the words from the box.**

Beach View Hotel,
10 Pebble lane,
Dorset,
DT1 XF2

12ᵗʰ August, 2014
Dear
How are you?
Love,

1 _____

2 _____ Mia,

3 _____ I'm fine.

We're staying at the Beach View Hotel in Dorset and it's great! I'm starting a shell collection. I got lots yesterday. I went to the beach and saw them on the sand. The best one is beautiful and pink. I think it's my best shell yet. I'm having a great time on holiday. It's hot and sunny. Tomorrow we're going on a hike and maybe to the cinema in the evening.

When I get home, I'll bring my photos and shells round to show you.

4 _____

Beth

24 **Write an informal letter to a friend. Tell your friend about a hobby. Here are some ideas:**

a healthy hobby   a creative hobby   a hobby that helps you learn

_____

_____

_____

_____

_____

_____

_____

_____

_____

25 **Read and circle y and igh.**

fly

try

light

high

my

picture

cute

true

sky

fight

night

26 **Underline the words with y and igh. Then read aloud.**

1 Birds fly high in the sky.

2 I watch the moon at night.

27 **Connect the letters. Then write.**

1 li   y   **a** _ _ _

2 m   ght   **b** _ _ _ _ _

3 fl   y   **c** _ _

164
28 **Listen and write.**

Let's ¹ _____,

Let's ² _____.

Let's ³ _____

And ⁴ _____

The ⁵ _____

At ⁶ _____!

29 **Complete the dialogues with forms of bad, good and old.**

1

A: Carol is _____ at chess.

B: Yes. But Henry is _____ Carol.

A: That's true. But I'm _____ of all.

2

A: Sean is a _____ singer.

B: I know! But Chris is _____ Sean.

A: Yes. But Brian is _____ singer of all.

3

A: Patty's grandma is 90. That's really

_____.

B: Yes, but Marge's grandma is _____

that. She's 98.

A: I know and Randy's grandma is

_____ of all. She's over a hundred!

30 **Answer about your family. Write complete sentences.**

1 Who's the best singer? _____

2 Who's the worst singer? _____

3 Who's the best dancer? _____

4 Who's the worst dancer? _____

5 Who's the oldest person? _____

31 **Read and circle.**

1 In the 19th century, dolls **was / were** made of china.

2 Football was **give / given** rules for the first time.

3 Girls **use to / used to** embroider cushions.

4 Collecting butterflies **was / were** a popular hobby.

Learning New Things

unit 9

 Solve the puzzle. Write the words in the boxes.

Across →

1
_____ like a rock star

2
draw _____ books

3
_____

4
make a _____

Down ↓

5
_____ a cake

6
build a _____

7
play the _____

8
_____ like a
hip-hop artist

 What things can you do? Write.

_____

_____

3 Listen and write. Use the words from the box.

> bake draw learn show sing
> skateboard speak

Learning Is Fun!

Do you know how to ¹_____?
    It's so brilliant. It's so cool!
I can ²_____ you how to do it
    On Friday after school.

It's fun to learn new things,
Like how to ³_____
    Or ⁴_____ or
        ⁵_____!
I wish I had a lot more free time.
I would try to ⁶_____ everything!

I'd like to learn to speak English.
"It's hard!" my friends all say.
But I think it's really interesting.
I'd like to ⁷_____ it well one day.

Chorus

Do you want
to learn English?

Yes!

4 What activities are amazing, dangerous and difficult? Write.

1 I think it's amazing to _____

_____.

2 I think it's dangerous to _____

_____.

3 I think it's difficult to _____

_____.

5 **Read. Then circle.**

The Best in the Class

Christina and Sam are walking home from school. They see Jake, a boy from Sam's class, in the park. He's really good at playing the guitar. Sam can't play the guitar but he'd like to learn. Jake tries to teach Sam to play the guitar. Sam isn't very good. Christina thinks Sam is terrible at playing the guitar.

1 Jake is in Sam's **class** / **football team**.

2 He is good at playing the **piano** / **guitar**.

3 Sam **can** / **can't** play the guitar.

4 He **would** / **wouldn't** like to learn how to play the guitar.

5 Sam **is** / **isn't** very good at playing the guitar.

6 **Write about you.**

I'd like to learn how to _____.

I'm good at _____.

I'm not very good at _____.

What happens next in the story? Use these ideas or think of your own.

1 Sam practises every day and learns how to play the guitar very well.

2 Sam goes home and plays video games.

3 Jake teaches Sam to play the guitar very well.

7 **Listen and stick. Then write.**

learn to dance   learn to draw   learn to play tennis   learn to skateboard

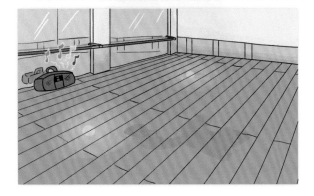

1 _____

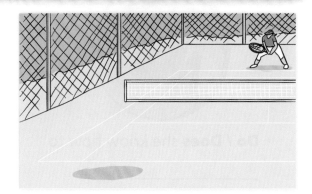

2 _____

3 _____

4 _____

8 **Look at 7. Complete the questions and write answers.**

1 What would he _____

_____?

_____

2 What would she _____

_____?

_____

3 What would she _____

_____?

_____

4 What would she _____

_____?

_____

Language in Action

9 **Look. Then circle and complete.**

1

Do / Does she know how to

_____?

_____. Her cakes
taste delicious.

2

Do / Does you know how to

_____?

_____. But I can
play tennis.

3

Do **he / they** know how to

_____?

_____. They're
building one right now.

4

Does **we / she** know how to

_____?

_____. But she speaks
English very well.

10 **Write the questions and answers.**

1 What does he think of snowboarding? _____ (fun)

2 What do you think of making websites? _____ (boring)

3 _____ They think it's difficult.
(dancing)

4 _____ She thinks it's amazing.
(drawing comic books)

11 **Read and complete.**

bones   brain   joints   muscle   organs   skeleton

Our body is an amazing machine. The ¹_____ support the frame. They make up the body's ²_____ and they protect the important ³_____ inside our bodies. Different ⁴_____, such as our shoulders, knees and elbows allow the frame to be flexible. These are covered with ⁵_____, which pulls the body in different directions. All of the different parts of the body are amazing but none of them can work without one thing – the ⁶_____.

12 **Read and number the paragraphs in order. Then listen and check.**

A If the tennis player is good, she finds the correct position and hits the ball with <u>precision</u>. If the tennis player isn't very good, she misses the ball.

B The tennis player's muscles <u>contract</u> to make the bones and joints of her legs and arms move. Everything magically moves together.

C A tennis player is standing at the end of a tennis court. She can see a ball coming toward her and she wants to hit it.

D The message travels down all the nerves and reaches the muscles. All the muscles get the message at the same time and get ready for <u>motion</u>.

E The tennis player's brain creates a message. It says something like, "Hey, muscles, this ball is coming my way – I really need to get into the correct position to hit it." Her brain sends the message to all her nerves, telling them that she wants to hit the ball.

13 **Look at 12. Correct the sentences.**

1 Your body tells your nerves that you want to move.

_____

2 Your joints send messages to your muscles.

_____

3 Your bones contract and get ready for motion.

_____

4 Your organs and joints move together.

_____

5 If you aren't a very good tennis player, you can hit the ball with precision.

_____

14 **Look at 12. Match the three underlined words to a definition.**

1 movement   _____

2 get smaller   _____

3 exactly right   _____

Think about your body. Complete the sentences.

THINK BIG

1 Without _____

_____

_____.

2 It's amazing that _____

_____

_____.

15 **Read, complete and match the offers.**

a _____ (I/put) some things in my bag if you like.

b _____ (I/give/you) mine. I had that lesson this morning.

c Really? _____ (I/open) a window, then.

d I don't know. _____ (I/help/you) look for them.

e Never mind. _____ (I/show/you) how to do it.

1 Mum, where are my favourite socks?

2 Wow, it's really hot in here.

3 I haven't got my Geography book with me!

4 My bag is really heavy.

5 I want to play this game but I don't know how.

16 **Read, choose and complete the decisions. Use will.**

| ask Mum buy get him give it tidy it watch |

1 My bedroom is really messy. _____ at the weekend.

2 I forgot about Tom's birthday. _____ a present later.

3 I haven't got any homework tonight. _____ a DVD instead.

4 My bike is really small now. _____ for a new one.

5 These T-shirts are both really nice but I think _____ the red one.

6 There's a cat in our back garden. _____ some milk.

17 **Put the words in the right order.**

1 carry I 'll bag your you for

_____

2 buy ball them 'll a new/I

_____

3 'll I eat sandwich a

_____

4 won't go to I school today

_____

5 go shopping 'll today I

_____

6 learn to I play another instrument musical 'll

_____

18 **Complete the mini dialogues with your own ideas. Begin with I'll....**

1 **Friend:** I don't like this programme. It's really boring.

   You: _____

2 **You:** Mum! I've cut my leg badly!

   Mum: Oh no! _____

3 **Dad:** You didn't do well in that exam!

   You: _____

4 **Waiter:** Would you like to order something?

   You: _____

5 **Friend:** I'm going to a concert tonight. Do you want to come?

   You: _____

19 Read and complete.

> average   exhibition   genius   Professional   talent

1 _____ musicians play music for money.

2 Tamara doesn't play really well or really badly, she's just _____.

3 Greta is a brilliant ballet dancer. She's got a lot of _____.

4 There's an _____ of Aztec art at the Metropolitan Museum.

5 Martin is only five and he knows so many things. I think he's a _____.

180

20 **Listen, read and match. Put the sentences in the correct place.**

A He isn't just a genius, though. He's kind and helpful, too.

B Some experts think young children can't be professional artists.

C His talent for playing the guitar showed when he was just four.

1   Yuto Miyazawa was a professional musician when he was only eight years old! **1** ☐ He was on TV and performed at Madison Square Garden. He even played with famous musicians like Ozzy Osbourne, Les Paul and G.E. Smith.

2   Gregory Smith could read at two years old. He started university at the age of ten and, by the time he was sixteen, had several degrees, including one in Maths. **2** ☐ Gregory uses his intelligence to help other people.

3   Aelita Andre could draw before she could walk. People were interested in her paintings when she was just two. At the age of four, she had her first exhibition in New York. **3** ☐ Nevertheless, all her paintings sold out in the first two weeks.

21 **Look at 20. Read and answer.**

1 Where did Yuto perform?

_____

2 Who did Yuto play with?

_____

3 How did Gregory get his degrees?

_____

4 What happened at Aelita's exhibition?

_____

22 **Find and write the words from 20.**

1 ngesiu _____

2 laettn _____

3 xebihtonii _____

4 frposesnoila _____

5 veagrae _____

Imagine what Yuto, Gregory and Aelita would say and write.

THINK BIG

1 **You:** Would you like to learn how to play another instrument?
Yuto: _____

2 **You:** Do you always like playing the guitar?
Yuto: _____

3 **You:** What do you think of playing with famous musicians?
Yuto: _____

4 **You:** Painting is really difficult. Do you think it's easy?
Aelita: _____

5 **You:** Do you ever play with people your own age?
Gregory: _____

Look and complete the review. Use the words from the box.

Reviewed by ¹_____

★ ★ ★ ☆

A Great ²_____ for Everyone!

Kara Makes a Robot is a ³_____ film. I watched it last ⁴_____ and I really liked it. It isn't a long film. It's only about eighty minutes but there is a lot of great ⁵_____ in it.

It's about a girl named Kara. She ⁶_____ a robot. At first, they are friends but soon the robot starts doing silly things. It's very funny and exciting. I don't want to tell you too much. You should watch it for ⁷_____.

Kara Makes a Robot is a great film and I ⁸_____ it to everyone!

| acting |
| builds |
| Film |
| filmgirl123 |
| funny |
| night |
| recommend |
| yourself |

Write a review of a film, book or TV show you like.

Reviewed by _____

_____

_____

_____

_____

_____

_____

_____

_____

_____

25 **Read and circle ew, ey and e_e.**

new   grey   hey

stew   bake   eve

those   stay

few   they   these

26 **Underline the words with ew, ey and e_e. Then read aloud.**

1 I've got a few of these grey scarves.

2 Hey, they've got a new board game.

27 **Connect the letters. Then write.**

1	th	ew	**a** _ _ _	
2	f	ese	**b** _ _ _ _ _	
3	n	ey	**c** _ _ _ _	
4	pr	ew	**d** _ _ _	

28 **Listen and write.**

185

¹ _____ three are

² _____ !

They eat ³ _____

And wear ⁴ _____ , too!

29 **Look at the chart. Write questions and answers.**

What do they think of... ?			
Luisa	interesting	amazing	boring
Martin	interesting	cool	fun

1 What does Luisa think of drawing comic books?

_____

2 _____

They think it's interesting.

3 What does Martin think of singing like a rock star?

_____

30 **Answer the questions in complete sentences.**

1 Does Phil know how to speak Chinese? (no/but/speak Spanish)

_____

2 What would they like to learn how to do? (build a robot)

_____

3 What does she want to learn how to do? (dance like a hip-hop artist)

_____

31 **Read and match.**

1 What would you like for dessert?

2 There's so much housework to do!

3 Oh, no... I feel really ill.

4 I'm going to a concert tonight.

a Ellie Goulding? I love her! I'll come with you.

b Don't worry. I'll take the children to school.

c I'll help you finish it.

d I'll have chocolate cake, please.

1 **Make guesses about Ben and ✓ the answers.**

Look at the happy and sad faces on Ben's calendar. Ben thinks some days are the best. He thinks some days are the worst.

1 What's Ben like?

☐ friendly   ☐ funny

☐ good at chess   ☐ good at sports

☐ serious   ☐ clever

2 What would Ben like to do?

☐ have a party   ☐ learn to snowboard

☐ learn to play chess   ☐ play video games

☐ watch fireworks   ☐ watch TV

Sun	Mon
31st Dec NEW YEAR'S EVE ☺ ☺ ☺	**1**st Jan ?
7th LEARN HOW TO ☹ ☹ ☹	**8**th MEET FRIENDS SHARE COLLECTION ☺ ☺

2 **Write on Ben's calendar. Write a hobby or things for Ben to learn on the tenth and the thirteenth.**

Make a guess about these two days.

3 **Look at the calendar. Make guesses and write the answers.**

1 What's Ben going to do on Monday?

_____

2 What special day is on Saturday the sixth?

_____

BEN'S CALENDAR

Tues	Wed	Thurs	Fri	Sat
2nd MEET FRIENDS SHARE COLLECTION ☺ ☺	**3rd** PRACTISE THE PIANO ☹ ☹	**4th** LEARN TO PLAY ☺ ☺ ☺	**5th** BAKE MUM'S BIRTHDAY CAKE ☺ ☺ ☺	**6th** ?
9th PRACTISE FOOTBALL ☹ ☹ ☹	**10th** ? _____ ☺ ☺ ☺	**11th** MAKE A WEBSITE ☺ ☺ ☺	**12th** LEARN TO PLAY BADMINTON ☹ ☹	**13th** ? _____ ☹ ☹ ☹

The best!

The worst!

4 **What do you think of Ben? Would you like to be Ben's friend? Write a letter about Ben to your parents. Begin:**

Dear Mum and Dad,

I've got a new classmate. His name is Ben. _____

_____

_____

_____

_____

_____

_____

_____

_____

Who is **taller**, Chris or Tom?	Chris is **taller than** Tom.

old	→	old**er**
big	→	big**ger**
heavy	→	heav**ier**

1 **Read. Write the answers.**

1 What is bigger? An elephant or a cat?

An elephant is _____ a cat.

2 What is heavier? A notebook or a computer?

A computer is _____ a notebook.

3 Who is older? Your grandmother or your aunt?

_____

4 Who is taller? Your brother/sister or your father?

_____

5 What is smaller? A baseball or a basketball?

_____

My sister's hair is longer than **my hair**.	My sister's hair is longer than **mine**.
My sister's hair is longer than **your hair**.	My sister's hair is longer than **yours**.

2 **Circle the correct words.**

1 **Your / Yours** backpack is heavy. But my backpack is heavier than **your / yours**.

2 **Their / Theirs** hair is long. But my hair is longer than **their / theirs**.

3 **Her / Hers** brother is younger than **my / mine**.

4 **Our / Ours** classroom is bigger than **their / theirs** classroom.

5 **My / Mine** friend is taller than Shaun's.

6 **He / His** shoes are smaller than **her / hers** shoes.

| **Where** is | he/she | going after school? | He/She | is going to football practice. |
| **What** are | you | doing tonight? | We | are watching a DVD at home. |

1 **Look. Write What or Where. Answer the questions.**

walk the dog

visit the dentist

1 _____ is she doing after school today?

She _____.

2 _____ are they going on Saturday?

They _____.

play video games

go to the shopping centre

3 _____ is he doing tonight?

He _____.

4 _____ are you going tonight?

We _____.

| **How often** does | he/she | have a guitar lesson? | **How often** do | you/they | go to school? |

2 **Circle the correct questions. Write the answers.**

1 **How often do / How often does** they do the dishes?

Mon | Tues

_____ a week.

2 **How often do / How often does** she visit her cousins?

Sun

_____ a week.

What **would** you **like**?			I'**d like** some soup.		I'd like ⟶ I would like
What **would**	he/she	**like**?	He'**d**/She'**d**	**like** yoghurt.	He'd/She'd like ⟶ He/She would like

1 **Look. Write questions. Write the answers.**

1 What would she like for breakfast?

_____ eggs on toast.

2 What _____ for a snack?

_____

3 _____

_____ for dessert?

_____

> ### Favourite Food Survey
> **1 Stacy:** eggs on toast for breakfast
> **2 Martin:** steamed buns for a snack
> **3 Stacy and Martin:** yoghurt and watermelon for dessert

	you				I				I	
Would	he/she	**like to try** some curry?	**Yes,**	we	**would.**	**No,**	we	**wouldn't.**
	they			he/she			he/she	
				they			they	

2 **Complete the dialogue. Use the correct form of do, would or like.**

1 **A:** Does Paula like Mexican food?

B: Yes, _____.

A: _____ she _____ to try some chili?

B: Yes, she would. She loves chili.

2 **A:** Do you like hot drinks?

B: No, _____.

A: Would you like to try some lemonade?

B: No, _____. Thanks anyway.

I		I	
You		You	
He/She	**should** eat healthy food.	He/She	**shouldn't** stay up late.
We		We	
They		They	

1 **Write sentences with should and shouldn't. Use the ideas in the boxes.**

1 I've got a fever.

_____

_____

> go to school today
>
> rest

2 Her tooth hurts.

_____

_____

> go to the dentist
>
> eat so many sweets

3 Ted fell and hurt his knee.

_____

_____

> go to basketball practice
>
> see the school nurse

4 Some children always feel tired.

_____

_____

> watch so much TV
>
> get more exercise

I		**myself.**
You		**yourself.**
He/She	should take care of	**himself/herself.**
We		**ourselves.**
They		**themselves.**

2 **Look at 1. Complete the sentences. Use herself, himself, themselves or yourself.**

1 You should take care of _____.

2 She should take care of _____.

3 He _____.

4 They _____.

> **How many** chimpanzees were there 100 years ago?

> There **were** more than one million. But now there **are** only about 200,000.

1 **Complete the sentences.**

Animal	Habitat	Population in the Past	Population Now
Mexican walking fish	streams and ponds in Mexico	a lot	almost none

¹_____ Mexican walking fish ²_____ in Mexico now?

³_____ a lot of Mexican walking fish in Mexican streams and ponds in the past?

Now, ⁴_____ almost none. In the past, ⁵_____ a lot.

> **Why** are chimpanzees endangered?

> They're endangered **because** people are moving into their habitat.

2 **Answer the questions. Use the information from the box and because.**

> their habitat's polluted
>
> people are keeping them as pets

1 Why is the Egyptian tortoise endangered?

It's endangered _____

_____ .

2 Why are Andean flamingos endangered?

_____

_____ .

Did people **have** cars in 1950?	Yes, they **did**.
Did people **have** cars in 1900?	No, they **didn't**. They travelled by horse and carriage or by train.
Before TV, what **did** people **use to do** for entertainment at night?	They **used to listen** to the radio.

1 **Read. Then answer the questions. Use did or didn't, do or don't, use or used.**

Then and Now

1930's – People usually listened to the radio. They didn't own TVs.

Today – People sometimes listen to the radio. Most people watch TV.

1950's – People wrote letters by hand.

Today – Many people write letters on the computer.

1970's – Young people played outdoor games, like hide and seek.

Today – Many people, young and old, play video games.

1 Did people listen to the radio years ago?

Yes, _____ because they didn't have TVs.

Do people listen to the radio now?

Yes, _____ but they usually watch TV.

2 Did people use to write letters on the computer a long time ago?

_____

Do they write letters on the computer now?

_____

3 Before video games, what _____ young people

_____ to do for fun?

They _____ to play hide and seek outdoors.

When **are**	you	**going to have** the party?	I	**am going to have** it on Monday.
	they		We	**are going to have** it on Monday.
			They	
When **is**	he/she	**going to visit** Grandma?	He/She	**is going to visit** her next month.
Are you/they going to visit Grandma **on the ninth**?			Yes, **on the ninth**.	
Is he/she going to visit Grandma **on the fifth**?			No, **on the ninth**.	

1 **Complete the questions and answers. Use going to and the words from the box.**

> fourth   second   third   twenty-second

1

give a present 2nd July

When _____ your dad _____ to your mum?

On the _____.

2

watch a parade 22nd April

When _____ they _____ a parade?

_____

3

wear different clothes 4th July

When _____ you _____ different clothes?

_____

4

have a party 3rd July

When _____ you _____ a party?

_____

2 **Look and write.**

1 fourteenth ____   **2** eighth ____   **3** thirtieth ____   **4** first ____

Katie is a **good** chess player.	My brother's paintings are **bad**.
Katie is a **better** chess player **than** Jeff.	My sister's paintings are **worse than** his.
Katie is **the best** chess player in the class.	My paintings are **the worst** of all.

1 **Look and complete the sentences.**

1 **(big)**

	Number of shells
John	85
Mike	250
Sally	1000

John loves collecting shells. His collection is ¹_____. Mike's collection is ²_____ John's. But Sally has got ³_____ in the whole class. She started when she was six.

2 **(good)**

	Wins
Ella	10
Stephanie	4
Tania	6

Ella is good at video games. She is ¹_____ in the class. Stephanie is a ²_____ video game player. But Tania practises a lot. She's ³_____ Stephanie.

3 **(bad)**

	Losses
The Bears	5
The Tigers	3
The Lions	4

The Bears, Tigers and Lions are popular baseball teams but they are not having a good year. The Bears team is ¹_____ of the three teams this year. The Lions are ²_____ than the Tigers. But the Tigers are pretty ³_____, too.

2 **Look and match.**

1 He's good   **a** good at climbing trees.

2 She's not very   **b** are bad at football.

3 They   **c** at music.

Do you **know how to play** the piano?			Yes, I do. / No, I don't.	
What would	you	like to learn how to do?	I'd	like to **learn how to play** the piano.
	he/she		He'd/She'd	
	they		They'd	

1 **Read. Then answer the questions. Use the words from the box.**

> bake a cake   make a website   sing like a rock star

1 Jeff and Tina are going to have singing lessons next year. What would they like to learn?

_____

2 Sue loves cakes. She's having a baking class now. What would she like to learn?

_____

3 Bryan loves computers. He's having a web-design class now. What would he like to learn?

_____

What do you **think of** ballet?	I think it's boring.
What does he **think of** hip-hop music?	He thinks it's cool.

2 **Complete the dialogues.**

1 **A:** What do _____

_____ ?

B: I _____ it's cool.

2 **A:** What does _____

_____ ?

B: She _____ it's a lot of fun.

– 5 questions –

 Listen and look. There is one example.

Getting Ready for School

Time Susan woke up: _7:30_

1 What she's having for breakfast: _____

2 How she's getting to school: _____

3 What homework she did for today: _____

4 What she's doing after school: _____

5 Her chore for today: _____

Young Learners English Practice Movers: Listening B

– 5 questions –

Listen and look. There is one example.

What is Martin's hobby?

A ☐

B ☐

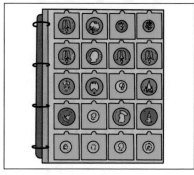

C ☑

1   What does Jane like doing?

A ☐

B ☐

C ☐

2   Which instrument does Anthony know how to play?

A ☐

B ☐

C ☐

3   What is the boy's favourite sport?

A ☐

B ☐

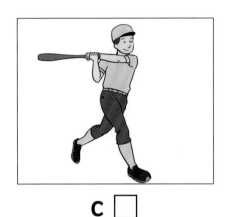

C ☐

4   What is the class going to do?

A ☐

B ☐

C ☐

5   What are they going to do later on?

A

B ☐

C ☐

– 6 questions –

Look and read. Write *yes* or *no*.

Examples

The dog knows how to ride a skateboard. _____ *yes* _____

The little boy knows how to ride a bicycle. _____ *no* _____

Questions

1 The girls know how to play tennis.   _____

2 The man can sing well.   _____

3 The bird knows how to talk.   _____

4 The woman is going to cross the street.   _____

5 A parade is coming.   _____

6 You can see fireworks in the sky.   _____

Young Learners English Practice Movers: Reading & Writing B

– 6 questions –

Look and read. Choose the correct words and write them on the lines.

a slide

chess

a guitar

a birthday cake

actors

a comic book

a video game

a robot

Example

This is a game you play on a computer or TV screen.

a video game

Questions

1 This is a musical instrument with strings.

2 These are the people in a play or film.

3 This is a game you play on a board by moving pieces.

4 This is a book that tells a story with pictures and speech bubbles.

5 This is a machine which does work for people.

6 This is something people often eat on their birthdays.

– 5 questions –

Read the text and choose the best answer.

Paul is talking to his friend Vicky.

Example

Vicky: Hi, Paul. What are you doing?

Paul: A   I'm fine, thank you.

  B   I had a party.

  Ⓒ   I'm making a cake.

Questions

1   **Vicky:**   What is it for?

Paul: A   It's for my parents' anniversary.

  B   On the last day of the year.

  C   It's two days until Mother's Day.

2 **Vicky:** Would you like some help?

  Paul: A OK. What time?

           B Sure, I would love to.

           C That would be great.

3 **Vicky:** What would you like me to do?

  Paul: A You can beat the eggs.

           B No thanks, I don't like eggs.

           C Two eggs are better than one.

4 **Vicky:** Should I use this bowl?

  Paul: A It's not as big as the other one.

           B No, use the bigger one.

           C Because I like it.

5 **Vicky:** And then what are we going to do?

  Paul: A Mix everything and put it in the oven.

           B Flour, eggs and milk.

           C The oven is hot now.

6 **Vicky:** When will it be finished?

  Paul: A Every once in a while.

           B In about an hour.

           C It lasts a long time.

 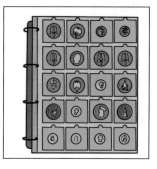  

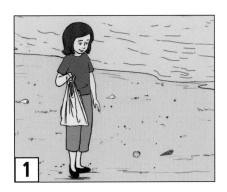

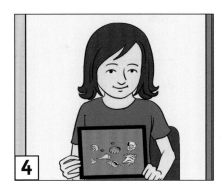

Extra Verb Practice

Base Form	Simple Past	Base Form	Simple Past
ask	_____	fly	_____
_____	baked	_____	got
be	_____	give	_____
_____	began	_____	went
bring	_____	grow	_____
_____	built	_____	had
buy	_____	hear	_____
_____	called	_____	helped
catch	_____	hit	_____
_____	celebrated	_____	held
change	_____	hope	_____
_____	came	_____	kept
cook	_____	kill	_____
_____	cut	_____	knew
destroy	_____	learn	_____
_____	did	_____	left
draw	_____	like	_____
_____	drank	_____	listened
drive	_____	live	_____
_____	ate	_____	looked
explain	_____	lose	_____
_____	fell	_____	loved
feed	_____	make	_____
_____	felt	_____	met
fight	_____	move	_____
_____	found	_____	needed

Base Form	Simple Past	Base Form	Simple Past
perform	_____	tell	_____
_____	planned	_____	thought
play	_____	throw	_____
_____	put	_____	travelled
read	_____	try	_____
_____	realised	_____	turned
rest	_____	understand	_____
_____	rode	_____	used
ring	_____	visit	_____
_____	ran	_____	waited
say	_____	wake up	_____
_____	saw	_____	walked
sell	_____	want	_____
_____	sent	_____	washed
sing	_____	watch	_____
_____	sat	_____	wore
skateboard	_____	worry	_____
_____	slept	_____	wrote
snowboard	_____	yell	_____
_____	spoke		
stand	_____		
_____	started		
stay up	_____		
_____	swam		
take	_____		
_____	talked		

My Pen Pal

I'd like to tell you about my

pen pal. _____ name is
　　　　　　(His/Her)

_____ .
(name)

_____ lives in
(He/She)

_____ .
(city, country)

1

He/She likes _____
　　　　　　　　(activity)

and _____ .
　　　(activity)

_____ wants to visit me here
(He/She)

in _____ , too!
　(where I live)

4

_____ loves eating

(name)

_____ food.

(adjective)

favourite dish is _____ .

(His/Her) (food)

(He/She) eats it _____ .

(how often)

I'd like to try it, too!

2

_____ has got

(name)

_____ hair.

(adjective)

hair is _____ .

(His/Her) (adjective)

(He/She) is really _____ .

(adjective)

3

sore eyes

ate too many sweets

have got a cold

sore throat

have got a cough

used the computer too much

stomachache

played too many video games

have got allergies from playing outside

sneezing

drank too much lemonade

watched too much TV

ate too many sweets

have got a cold

have got a cough

used the computer
too much

played too many
video games

have got allergies from
playing outside

drank too much lemonade

watched too much TV

sore eyes

sore throat

stomachache

SCHOOL TALENT SHOW

Wednesday, 9th May

6:00 P.M.–7:30 P.M.

School Auditorium

Vote for the best talent!

Sign up to perform by Friday, 4th May.

4 My BIG ENGLISH
World

My name: _____

My age: _____

My address: _____

My family: _____

ME →

FOLD

ENGLISH
AROUND ME

Look around you. Paste or draw things with English words. Write everyday words and sentences.

Everyday Words

Everyday Sentences

Henry's Chocolate

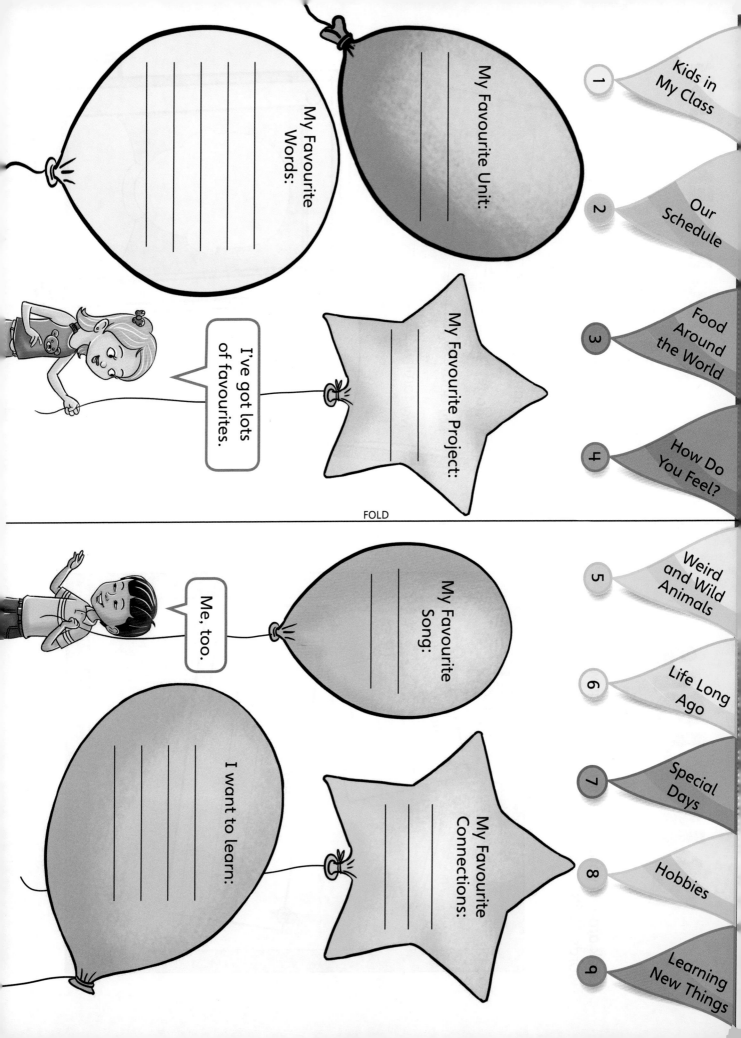

Pearson Education Limited
Edinburgh Gate
Harlow
Essex CM20 2JE
England
and Associated Companies throughout the world.

www.pearsonelt.com/bigenglish

© Pearson Education Limited 2015

Authorised adaptation from the United States edition entitled Big English, 1st Edition, by Mario Herrera and Christopher Sol Cruz. Published by Pearson Education Inc. © 2013 by Pearson Education, Inc.

The right of Mario Herrera and Christopher Sol Cruz to be identified as the authors of this Work have been asserted by them in accordance with the Copyright, Designs and Patents Act 1988.

First published 2015
Thirteenth impression 2023

ISBN: 978-1-4479-9441-1

Set in Heinemann Roman

Editorial and project management by hyphen S.A.

Printed in Slovakia by Neografia

Acknowledgements

The publisher would like to thank the following for their kind permission to reproduce their photographs:

(Key: b-bottom; c-centre; l-left; r-right; t-top)

Age Fotostock Spain S.L.: 140tl, Jeff Greenough 27, Jochen Tack 113l; **Alamy Images:** Amanda Ahn 83c, Anyka 104tc, Arco Images / Wegner, P. 63 (elephant sticker), Jon Berkeley 60tc, 71tl, Blend Images 38, 90tl, blickwinkel 65tl, Anders Blomqvist 90bl, James Boardman 12tl, 12bl, Brand Z 74 (oil lamp), 89l, Collection 50, Design Pics Inc 60t, 63b, 71tr, dpa picture alliance archive 65bl, Chuck Eckert 16tc, Alan Edwards 122tr, David R Frazier 118/4, 131l, 133b, Raga Jose Fuste 95, GL Archive 74 (washing clothes by hand), Jeff Greenberg 118/6, 122bl, Ernie Janes 109r, Jeff Morgan 109cl, johnrochaphoto 104tr, 133tr, Ladi Kirn 140bl, Robert Landau 74 (traffic), H Lefebvre 74 (coal stove), Justin Leighton 90cr, Lordprice Collection 109l, Michael Newman 2r, David Page 16tl, 103, Ingolf Pompe 83br, RF Images 104bl, RGB Ventures LLC DBA Superstock 113r, RIA Novosti 83bc, H Armstrong Roberts 74 (listened to the radio), 89r, Pep Roig 79l, SAGAPhoto.com / Roux Olivier 118/2, 131r, Ian Shaw 2cr, Stock Illustrations Ltd 12br, The Africa Image Library 60bc, 64, Vintage Images 74 (horse and carriage), Stacy Walsh Rosenstock 90br, Wave Royalty Free / Design Pics Inc 74 (microwave), Sara Zinelli 12tr; **Corbis:** George D. Lepp 60c, 71bl, Reuters / Mick Tsikas 127bl; **DK Images:** Ian OLeary 63c, 71bc, 73c; **Fotolia. com:** allocricetulus 55cl, ameli k 104 (coin collection), 132br, anankkml 63 (tiger sticker), 71tc, Artranq 74 (electric light), Benicce 74 (mobile phone), bit24 55bl, Blend Images 2l, burakdemirezen 30 (h), 45tl, Jacek Chabraszewski 40, 104tl, CJPhoto 104 (doll collection), clearviewstock 104 (singer), DMM Photography Art 109cr, ExQuisine 30 (d), 45br, Fabio Lotti 63 (rhino sticker), 71br, Flowerpower 140tr, freestyleone 30 (f), Joe Gough 30 (c), 45tc, 45bl, haveseen 60b, 73t, jjpixs 19, kazakovmaksim 65br, Ivan Kmit 104 (shells), Konstantin Li 122br, Monkey Business 16bl, 119r, nina dezhda 30 (g), Anna Omelchenko 119l, poonsap 30 (e), rpo7 65tr, Schlierner 55r, Uryadnikov Sergey 63t, 69, WavebreakmediaMicro 88, Edward Westmacott 55tl, Alexander Yakovlev 118/8, zest_marina 30 (a), 45tr; **Getty Images:** KidStock 3r, Amos Morgan 3l; **Glow Images:** Radius Images 17, Superstock 74 (use phone with an operator); **Imagestate Media:** John Foxx Collection 118/3, 132bl; **PhotoDisc:** Alan D Carey 73b; **Reuters:** 127r; **Rex Features:** Sinopix 127tl; **Shutterstock.com:** Peter Albrektsen 104 (car collection), 133tl, AVAVA 104 (video game), bds 74 (washing machine), bikerider london 74 (listen to mp3), bikeworldtravel 90cl, Franck Boston 39, 41, Steve Bower 7, Cheryl Casey 105, Sam Chadwick 79tr, Shchipkova Elena 2cl, Mike Flippo 132t, fusebulb 52bl, Warren Goldswain 13, 118/1, 131c, Chris Harvey 113c, Charlie Hutton 79br, Innershadows Photography 118/5, 122tl, Kamira 104br, Sebastian Kaulitzki 52tl, Lukasz Kurbiel 138, Lara65 104bc, Lebendkulturen.de 52br, nikkytok 52tr, Denis Radovanovic 142l, tacar 30 (b), Peter Weber 118/7, 142r, wormdog 57, yalayama 20; **SuperStock:** 16tr, Asia Images 16bc, Blend Images 90tr, Lisette Le Bon 140br, Stockbroker / Purestock 16br

Cover images: *Front:* **Shutterstock.com:** Lukasz Kurbiel c, Rudchenko Liliia l; **SuperStock:** Corbis r

All other images © Pearson Education

Every effort has been made to trace the copyright holders and we apologise in advance for any unintentional omissions. We would be pleased to insert the appropriate acknowledgement in any subsequent edition of this publication.

Illustrated by
Sean@KJA-Artists, Matt Latchford, Victor Moshopoulos, Zaharias Papadopoulos (hyphen) Jamie Pouge, Q2A Media Services and Christos Skaltsas (hyphen).